Post–War Europe Through the Eyes of Youth

Post–War Europe Through the Eyes of Youth

Alice Carlstedt Nelson

VANTAGE PRESS
New York

FIRST EDITION

Copyright © 2002 by Alice Carlstedt Nelson

Published by Vantage Press, Inc.
516 West 34th Street, New York, New York 10001

Manufactured in the United States of America
ISBN: 0-533-13980-5

Library of Congress Catalog Card No.: 01-130629

0 9 8 7 6 5 4 3 2 1

To the named and unnamed individuals in charge of the Lutheran World Federation, its National Lutheran Council Division of Student Services, and Lutheran Campus Ministry who sponsored and planned this trip and selected us to participate; to the European youth and their leaders who blessed us by sharing their struggles and hard-won victories with us, often to the point of sacrifice; and to the comrades who so enriched the trip and my life then and since.

To the Christ and His Church who made such sharing possible.

Contents

Acknowledgment

It was a pleasure to receive the endorsement of the Lutheran World Federation through a special friend, Dr. Daniel Martensen, until very recently of ELCA Headquarters, who was the U.S. representative of the Lutheran World Federation, and to be able to talk over with him matters related to this project as it progressed.

Foreword

It had been forty-five years between the time I closed my diary on our return trip to the U.S. in 1953 after our summer in Europe, and my opening it again in 1998.

There really didn't seem to be any reason to reread it. How could one forget! Twenty of us Lutheran Students Association members from colleges and universities around the country had been encouraged to apply, and were then selected, for the privilege of traveling in the European countries with a leader and his wife under the auspices of the Lutheran World Federation. We were all eager to meet each other and our fellow Lutheran students and were not disappointed. We had a memorable summer! We all had reasons, assigned or otherwise, to talk about it on various occasions on our return and most of us were able to share "Do you remember when . . . s" with others in the group in the first months and even years. But as new careers, marriages, and other life changes filled our time, we gradually drifted farther apart. The early death of Mary Ellerby, who had volunteered to be our group correspondent, did not help.

Unexpected reunions brought pleasure. Phil and I did not know that first day in New York or throughout the trip that a close friend of his was courting my sister and that he would end up at my home as groom's man for their wedding within the year. My husband and I found time to look up Marty on a trip to northern California. Beverly renewed our correspondence after she read my article in

Lutheran Women in 1983, thirty years after we parted. When husband Armour and I retired to Lindsborg, Kansas in 1990, I read Phil's name as being on the Bethany College Board and let him know I was here. We subsequently were able to get reacquainted when he came for Board meetings. We learned later that Dick was also in the audience, as representative for Carthage College, when Phil and I attended the installation of Bethany's new president, Christopher Thomforde. Ralph's cousin, Rev. Roger Anderson, was our pastor in Thousand Oaks, Ca, and Ralph and I had a wonderful visit when he came to see Roger. As Phil and I spread the word of our meetings to those we were in touch with, others began to say, "Hey! We all need a reunion!" Beverly began the search for the current addresses of the members of our group via Internet and Phil invited us to meet in St. Louis, with him making the local arrangements, with the time set for August 21–23, 1998, forty-five years after our summer together.

Less than a month before we met, Dick Preis was scheduled to give his *The Gospel According to Broadway* program, the first of a series of such original programs he has been giving around the country, in Lindsborg for the Missouri Lutheran Church Seniors (Saints Alive). Of course I had to attend and thoroughly enjoyed both the content of the program—music, meditations, and comedy—and seeing him again after all those years! [He gave the program again during our reunion in St. Louis, both for our sakes and for the public as a benefit for the Lutheran Students Association, and it was enjoyed by all.] I went home and just had to look up my '53 Diary. I was highly amused when I quickly came across the incident in which Dick had displayed his already well-developed comedic talents, though in a situation hardly to be chosen by him, as much as the rest of us enjoyed it. It was hard to put down the diary that night and I finished it the next day, being utterly intrigued by forgotten details.

One thing that did surprise me was the negative feelings we students and our leader, Reverend Seyda, expressed towards each others' ideas in the early part of the trip. He had been the leader of my branch of the Lutheran Student Association, and I had had a cordial relationship with him. It was his backing that brought me into the venture, and he would not have been asked to lead the trip had he not had a good reputation as a student leader. So no wonder I asked myself if I were suddenly playing the role of a protective big sister as I joined in opposing his views. I now believe that the change was, at least in part, due to the fact that all of us were in new and important roles, perhaps over-anxious to do and say what we most deeply believed. Guidance from Dr. Stendahl* whom we all highly respected, was probably crucial in our learning to relax and live more comfortably with each other. It occurs to me now that he might also have talked the situation over with Reverend Seyda. In any case, we seemed more willing to see the good in each other later in the trip.

The diary was such a small book that it was difficult

---

*As Stockholm Bishop and as Dean of Harvard Divinity School in the U.S. for a number of years, Dr. Stendahl had later dealings with some of our group. Four members mentioned in the biographies submitted for our 1998 reunion that he had made significant changes in their own lives through later encounters. I am excited about the fact that as I write this, Dr. Stendahl is scheduled to be the speaker for an ecumenical service in Lindsborg that will be the opening for the October Hyllnings-fest here, a biennial celebration of "Little Sweden in America,"'s Lindsborg's designative Swedish heritage.

to read. Hoping to reread it, I decided to type it up so that it would be easier to do so. My typing had not proceeded very far before our gathering in St. Louis, but I took it along and read a few pages to the group, finding that they seemed to enjoy it as much as I had. There were a lot of memories shared, though our time went all too quickly, but apparently no one had recorded memories in as much detail as I had. I knew as I stayed up night after night to write, that it was only because I had always been a night person. And I wasn't always up to it either. There was only one period when my entries were confined to only 4–5 lines per day. That was June 27–30, when we were in Norway. A couple of the few lines given to those days were about how tired and dirty I was and how fast our pace was; I needed sleep. On July 1, when I say I stayed up to catch up on my journal entries, I was obviously cutting them and Norway short. I am including most of Dick's article in the November issue of *The Campus Lutheran* that year, especially because he devotes a couple of paragraphs to that period. In more wakeful moments, I vividly recall our meeting with Bishop Bergrav in the most memorable of stav churches I have seen—in Telemark—and the Folke Museum and other sites in Oslo. Memories even include meeting a good friend Esther Olson from home on the street in Oslo.

I also regretted not being able to dwell on experiences during the period between July 27 and August 6: events relating to the uniqueness of the Evangelical Academy movement, Bielefeld, Cologne, visiting a legislative session in Bonn, Heidelberg, the Ulm Cathedral, Augsburg, unforgettable meetings with students and leaders in Munich, Insula, "the island of love" for Displaced Persons and Hitler's Eagle's Nest in Berchtesgaden—places I would like to recall in detail. Shall we all put out a revised edition of the story of our trip some day?

In response to requests from the group, I made copies of the material I had, and sent them out a few months after our reunion. Reading Tom Brokaw's World War II books, *The Greatest Generation,* and *The Greatest Generation Speaks,* recently, brought the Post-War Europe we knew back to me and warmed my heart. And I wondered if my account of our reconciling trip between Americans and Europeans might also warm the hearts of readers.

As I re-read this book for the purpose of proof-reading *after* our own September 11th horrifying disaster, I find myself being moved in new ways. I have greater sympathy for countries and people who were still living with the destroyed homes and lives and the fears remaining from *country-wide* destruction and ruins left by a World War taking place in their own lands. No wonder we felt the need for reconciliation with them, and were in awe of their efforts to rebuild lives as well as the still apparent ruins more than five years later. It comforted me now to remember the courage and faith with which they persisted.

It is with that hope that I submitted my story to Vantage Press and decided to sign the contract they offered me. As I won't be including all of Mary Ellerby's letter to us in early 1954, I at least want to close this with the last paragraph of her letter:

When we think of our trip, let's each one of us take a minute out and thank God again for giving us this opportunity to see our brothers in Christ and to pray that He may help us use this chance to His Glory, so that because we are led, someone else may be led by us to Christ, and because we are helped, our brothers in need across the sea will be helped.

All of us have called the trip a "life-changing" experience for us, and if this account can be used to help anyone else, I know that I speak for all of the group in thanking God for that.

Post–War Europe Through the Eyes of Youth

Itinerary of Lutheran World Federation Study Tour

1. June 19

Arrive Rotterdam, Holland. Dock. Take train to Amsterdam as a group at own discretion. Hourly trains take about an hour. Arrive 1800. Take taxi or streetcar to Hotel van Kooyk, Leidsekade 81, Tel. 30295. Dinner and breakfast included on bill. Bill paid as a group. Evening free. Canal ride is suggested.

2. June 20

Depart Amsterdam 0800 from Main Railroad Station on the Holland Scandinavian Express, III Class. Reserved seats. Arrive 0012 on June 21 in Copenhagen. Lunch can be purchased on dining car in Guilders, Marks, or dollars. Will cost about $1.50. The train will board the ferry at Frederecia, Denmark, at about 1930. If you can hold out that long, you can get a delicious Danish meal on board. A money changer will enter the train in Germany. It is a good idea to buy about $10 in Danish Kroner from him. You will be met by Danish students in white student caps in railroad station. You will not be permitted into the railroad station without the railroad ticket. Customs aboard the train en route.

3. June 21–25

Visit to Denmark. Lectures, tours, discussions, arranged by Miss Ragnhild Jeppesen, Medical student, and Mr. Kai-Eric Lindquist, Chairman of the SCM in Copenhagen.

4. June 26

Travel to Oslo. Depart from main railway station at 1300 on Scandinavienspiel. II Class, reserved seats. Famous Norwegian smörbröd (open-faced sandwiches) can be purchased on train at a special stop. Arrive 2250 Oslo. Met by Norwegian students in black student caps. (Customs via board the train en route.)

5. June 27–July 1

Visit to Norway. Lecture, tours, discussions arranged by Rektor Carl F. Wisloff, member Lutheran World Federation Student Commission, Pastor Sverrer Magelssen, Executive Secretary Studentenlaget, and pastor Svein Hanssen-auer, Executive Secretary Studentenforbundet.

6. July 2

Travel to Stockholm. Depart Oslo Ostbahnstation (East Railroad station—*not* West Railroad Station) at 0905. III Class, reserved seats. Arrive Stockholm 1810. Eat lunch on train, dinner in Stockholm. Met by students in white student caps. (Customs on en route train.)

7. July 3

Depart Stockholm 1100 by boat for Helsinki, II Class berth on boat reserved. Meals must be purchased on board. (Buying food for lunches before boarding ship a good idea.) Finnish visa necessary in order to leave the boat in Helsinki. Arrive 0800 July 4. Met by Finnish students with "pink" in their buttonholes.

8. July 4–9

Visit to Finland. Arranged by Mr. Risto Lehtonen, traveling Secretary, Finnish Student Christian Federation.

July 4

Arrival, sightseeing, and orientation. Evening with SCM students with lecture and free discussion.

July 5

Sunday morning worship in Tuusula Parish Church. The afternoon and evening in the Parish Institute in Jarvenpaa. Lecture and discussion.

July 6

Visits in Helsinki to Academic Institutes. Departure by train in evening to Teiniharju.

July 7–8

Join in camp at Teinijarju.

July 9

Arrival in Turku about noon. Visits to some places of historical interest and headquarters of Finnish Church.

9. July 9

Departure for Sweden 1900 from Turku Abo by II Class boat. Berth reservations.

10. July 10

Arrival in Stockholm 1000. The day spent in Stockholm, visiting church institutions.

11. July 11

Departure in morning for conference site. Train from main railway station. No reservations. Take train to Mursta, disembark, and take waiting bus to Lekmannaskolan at Sigtuna. Exact instructions will be given in Stockholm.

12. July 11–16

Scandinavian Conference with participants from Norway, Sweden, Finland, and Denmark, Chairman of the Conference, Pastor Krister Stendahl, lecturer at Uppsala University, assisted by Mr. Lars Thunberg, theology student and Miss Ingalill Hellman, student in languages and literature. Theme of the Conference: Christian Hope. Conference ends noon July 17. You are the guest of the Lutheran World Federation at the Conference.

13. July 17

Tour to Uppsala University, visit to parish.

14. July 18–23

The schedule for these days will be finally decided at the conference, depending upon the wishes of the participants. The first three days to be spent in visiting places in Sweden suggested by the Swedish Committee. Included will be a trip to Lund, Sweden, the scene of the formation of the Lutheran World Federation in 1947 and the home of the famous Lund Cathedral. Train tickets to Lund from Stockholm to be purchased individually in Sweden. Cost, about $9.00. The second three days are free for your personal travel in Scandinavia. If you have relatives to visit, this is the proper time to do it, unless you wish to come back to Scandinavia at the end of the summer. You will also have opportunities to visit the homes of students you met at the conference. This travel is at your own expense.

15. July 24

Reassembly at the main railway station in Copenhagen at 0845. Board of the Scandinavian-Italian Express at 0900, III Class, reserved seats. Arrive, Hannover, Germany, 1940. You will be met in Hannover by Miss Kathryn Markhus, who will accompany your entire German trip, managing the technical details for you. She will arrange for meals and rooms and pay for them out of a common fund to which you have already contributed.

16. July 25–28

Orientation to Germany by visit to Hannover. Introduction to German parish life, to youth situation in Germany and Lutheran World Federation. Visit to sites of Hannover Assembly of the Lutheran World Federation.

17. July 29

Beginning of eleven-day chartered bus tour of northern and southern Germany. Depart for Loccus Evangelical Academy 0900. Arrive 1030. Fifty kilometers. Briefing by Pastor Wischmann. Tour of Academy and Abbey. Depart for Espelkamp 1500. Arrive 1700. Seventy-five kilometers. Tour of Espelkamp and briefing on the refugee situation in Germany and its solution by Pastor Plantiko.

18. July 30

Depart 0900 for Bielefeld. Arrive 1030. 55) un. Spend the day touring the "Community of Love," being briefed on its history and services.

19. August 1

Depart 0830 for Koln. Arrive 1000 at Cathedral. Forty-five kilometers. Tour Cathedral. Depart for Bonn at 1100. Arrive Bonn 1200. Twenty-five kilometers. Afternoon tour of Bundestag, briefing on political parties. Depart Bonn at 1600, drive along Rhine. Dinner at St. Goar, near the Lorelei. Arrive Mainz at the University Student Home 2030. Visit to the new Albert Schweitzer student house, home of Studentengemeinde, Pastor Christian Semler, Student Pastor, host.

20. August 2

Church in Evangelical Chapel in the University 1000. Depart for Worms 1130. Forty-five kilometers. Arrive Worms 1230. Lunch. Tour scene of Luther's "Here I stand." Depart for Heidelberg 1500. Thirty-five kilometers. Arrive Heidelberg 1600. Report to Goldene Rose Hotel. Rest of afternoon and evening free to see city.

21. August 3

Depart Heidelberg 0830. Arrive Stuttgart 1100. one hundred and thirty-five kilometers. Briefings at Evangelical Hilfswerk on welfare work in Germany, by Miss Clara Anderson and others. Depart for Ulm 1600. Arrive 1800. Seventy-five kilometers. Dinner with Pralat Eichele. Tour Cathedral. Lecture on Lutherans and the Evangelical Church in Germany (Ekid).

22. August 4

Depart 0830 for Augsburg. Arrive 1000. Seventy-five kilometers. Visit to St. Anna Church, scene of the proclamation of the Augsburg Confession. Depart 1100 for Munich. Arrive 1200. Fifty kilometers. Tour of Munich. Interview with Bishop Meiser, Leading German Bishop. 1530, Lecture, Lutheran and the United Evangelical Lutheran Church in Germany, Pastor Katterfeld. Evening with the Studentengemeinde in the Student House.

23. August 5

Depart 0830 for Berchtesgaden. Arrive 1200. 140 kilometers. Lunch, tour of Insula, the "island of love" for Displaced Persons who cannot immigrate, under Hitler's Eagle's Nest. Depart 1700. Arrive 2130 at Student House, Munich.

24. August 6

Depart 0830 for Nurnberg. Arrive Valka D.P. Camp 1200. one hundred and sixty kilometers. Autobahn. Lunch at Valka. Tour of camp and briefing. Tour of Nurnberg. Depart 1730 for Stein Mother's Home. Arrive Stein 1800. Dinner. Briefing on the work by Dr. Nopitsch, Director.

25. August 7

Depart 0900 for Neuendettelsau. Arrive 0930. twenty kilometers. Tour of Neuendettelsau. Briefings on Inner Mission work, Foreign Mission, Theological Seminaries. Depart 1700 for Rothenburg, oldest city in Germany. Arrive 1830 at Boy's Home, being briefed on its work. Evening in Boy's Home.

26. August 8

Tour of the city, visit to Lutheran cathedral. Depart for Nurnberg 1100. Arrive 1300. Eighty-five kilometers. Lunch in Nurnberg. Report to Air France office at 1400. Bus to Airport 1415. Flight to Berlin by Air France 1530. Luggage limit, forty-four pounds. Arrive Berlin, 1730.

27. August 9–11

Visit to Bible Study Conference at Johannestift. The East Zone, problems and opportunities. Professor Martin Fischer in charge.

28. August 12–13

Tours of Berlin, seeing refugee screening, tourist sights, Oberkirchenrat Zimmermann in charge.

29. August 14–16

Flight from Berlin to Hamburg 1200, British European Airways. Arrive Hamburg 1326. Participate in Kirchentag under auspices of the Foreign Office of the Kirchentag. Stay in German homes.

30. August 16

Departure from Hamburg to Braunschweig by train. Tour conducted by Pastor Carl B. Mau, Jr., L.W.F. representative in Hannover. Departure for Hannover by car.

31. August 17

REST.

32. August 18–25

Departure for Göttingen. Conference begins at 2000 at Maria-spring, with German student representatives from all major Western Germany Universities. Pastor Dieter Andersen, Student Pastor, University of Göttingen, Chairman. Theme: *Christian Hope.*

33. August 25

Conference ends, trip to Göttingen to see University.

34. August 26

Free for personal travel. Meet in Rotterdam on the boat.

Participants 1953 European Study Tour and Schools Represented

1. Carlstedt, Alice: University of Chicago, Grad. R.N.
2. Dippold, Barbara Ann: Hartwick College, Oneonta, New York.
3. Ellerby, Mary: Lewis and Clark College, Portland, Oregon.
4. Fenske, Margaret: University of Minnesota, St. Paul, Minnesota.
5. Fieve, Ronald: University of Wisconsin, Grad. Med., Madison, Wisconsin.
6. Frieman, Charles: Columbia College, Brooklyn, New York.
7. Gammeter, Carolyn: University of Wisconsin, Grad. Med., Madison, Wisconsin.
8. Graham, Philip: Drake University, Des Moines, Iowa.
9. Knudten, Richard: Wittenberg College, Springfield, Ohio.
10. Lamp, Beverly: University of Texas, Grad., Austin, Texas.
11. Larson, Paul: Mansfield State Teachers College, Mansfield, Pennsylvania.
12. Mardorf, Jane: Iowa State Teachers College, Cedar Falls, Iowa.
13. Messerschmidt, Margaret: Brooklyn College, Brooklyn, New York.

14. Peterson, Ralph: University of Minnesota, Minneapolis, Minnesota.
15. Petrea, Margaret: Duke University, Durham, North Carolina, Grad. R.N.
16. Preis, Richard: University of Kansas, Grad., Lawrence, Kansas.
17. Samuelson, Frank: Northwestern University, Wilmette, Illinois.
18. Stoutland, Fred: St. Olaf College, Northfield, Minnesota.
19. Wertman, Carolyn: Brooklyn College, Brooklyn, New York.
20. Zacharias, Bonnie: Wartburg College, Waverly, Iowa.

21. LEADER: Seyda, Reverend Arthur: Pastor to Lutheran Students, University of Chicago, Northwestern University, Wilmette, Illinois.
22. Seyda, Mrs. Lorraine, Wife of Leader.

Prologue to Diary as Sent to Participants, October 10, 1998

Dear '53 Friends,

How good it was to see most of you in St. Louis in August! In fact, I thought it was downright exciting. I'm glad I kept a diary because I have been reliving a lot of details I would never have remembered had I not dug that out after hearing Dick's *The Gospel According to Broadway* in Lindsborg a couple of weeks before our reunion. I enjoyed typing up my entries and reliving it before our gathering and I have shared portions of it with a number of people since, including a bit of it with you in St. Louis.

I laughed the first night I worked on it as I read the incident on the boat involving Dick's Jerry Lewis act. I had just seen the theologian, actor, singer, and comedian. All that was missing that early day was the singer. *He hasn't changed,* I told myself. By the time I had gotten into my diary, I realized that I hadn't changed that much either. I know now that I am wordy and always have been, but I hadn't thought of it as being apparent in my graduate school days. I concluded, back in the days that I had to evaluate the assets and liabilities of student nurses, that our outstanding characteristics are likely to be both assets and liabilities in different situations—a paradox—and that has been true of my wordiness, but it is part of me.

A few of you asked for copies of my diary, saying you

would be glad to share in the cost of duplicating and mailing the forty-page "thing," so I have decided to send it to all of you. I'll let you know what it costs me per person and you can make a contribution or not; it won't matter that much to me whether you do or don't but if it makes you feel better . . . I am including our itinerary. Give me another six months and I could also give you fifty pages or so, probably, of notes on the presentations we listened to and our discussions, but that isn't likely.

All that I have deleted are a few comments about conflicts over what was happening at home or in my romance with Armour. I gave considerable thought to whether or not I should use Rev. Seyda's name because I don't want to dishonor it. But I decided to leave it as written because I think it is instructive to a reader about the kinds of disagreements that can readily happen, especially between generations, and because we were shown how to deal with that. I think it worked because the subject doesn't really come up later, and I even have some complimentary things to say about Rev. Seyda, whom I had liked as a friend before the trip and continued to like as long as I knew him.

I wondered, as I reread the diary, what the rest of you were doing at the times that I am repeatedly mentioning a certain few people. Does anyone else have similar accounts of what was going on with other sections of the group? It would be interesting to compare. I doubt it, because another of my qualifications for having kept such a diary is that I have always been a "late" person, though my "early bird" husband was able to gradually change that somewhat. But I normally went to bed between 12 A.M. and 1 A.M., and I am back to that pattern now. Who else would be sitting up writing in a diary at the ungodly hours that I was doing so? Though the lack of sleep was a bit much even for me!

Make what you want of it; I just hope it will bring back some great memories for all of you.

Love, Alice N.

Diary of Lutheran World Federation Study Tour to Europe, Summer of 1953

As recorded by Alice Carlstedt (now Nelson)

June 1, 6 P.M.

I am on the train for New York. I have slept in a different bed every night for the past week and feel somewhat oriented to my trip already by the constant changes: Monday—Aunt Elaine's; Tuesday—Marge's; Wednesday—Aunt Elaine's; Thursday—home at Sandstone; Friday—Aunt Caroline's; Saturday—Anne and Faisal's; tonight on the train. I spent a day with Mary at the Gillette O.P. Clinic and went to graduation at Augsburg—both Rhoda and Faith were *cum laude*. I spent a rough night my first night at home; everything hit me and I was depressed and anxious. [*Most of you knew that there had been a tragedy in my family during the year.*] I felt pretty tense and tied up over the prospect of being gone for so long, but I have better moments when I have confidence that God has many blessings in store through the summer. Most of all, I want to really face and accept myself before God as a sinner and to be won by His grace to a more joyous relationship with Him.

19

June 8, 2 A.M.

I arrived in New York, met Phil Graham as I registered at the hotel. So, we spent 1–8:30 sight-seeing, seeing the movie *Coronation*, and eating. I met some of the rest of the group tonight and like them all *very* much so far. We got our itinerary and it looks exciting. Some of us walked for miles this morning, then jumped into a taxi. At 8 A.M. we found a note asking for us to be at the National Lutheran Office at 7:30. We were about to take a taxi but fortunately found out it was just around the corner.

June 9:

A long-winded orientation today. It all sounds stupendous. Dr. Wick (Ruth) told us we would come back changed persons 'cause everyone always has, and I believe it!

June 10:

Am about to turn in for my first night at sea. A rope got tangled in the propeller so we sat in the harbor next to the Statue of Liberty from noon till about 7 P.M. before taking off. We watched a diver go down to fix it. I already have a sunburn but it looks worse than it feels.

June 12:

Quite a full day at sea. The weather has been calm and no one seasick yet. We stay up late and seem to keep busy all day; I don't think anyone is getting too much rest. There

We sailed both going and returning on Holland-American ships: the Zuiderkruis going over and the Groote Beer on our return. They looked much alike as both were special student sailings.

have been some tensions produced during our daily meetings; discussions and a Bible study. Some of us wonder if the group is pulling apart rather than drawing together; no one gets a chance to make himself fully heard or understood and others don't dare try to get a word in edgewise.

June 14, 12 Midnight:

I'm afraid we disgraced ourselves today. We held a Protestant service this morning, which was quite well-attended—further calling attention to our presence, I suppose. Tonight after Bible study, we clogged the hallways discussing the fact that we are all sinners, discussing the Sermon on the Mount much too noisily. Afterwards, Dick Preis, Margaret Petrea and I retired to the bar-room lounge to discuss divorce in connection with Matt. 5:31–32. (*I had had a long talk earlier with Rev. Seyda about WBS and his divorce, and Dick's parents were separated.*) We were gradually joined by others, including two Concordia Seminary students, Walt and Paul. Dick began to put on a silly act about United Lutheran Church vs. Mo. Synod. They dragged him out about Dr. Maier of the Lutheran Hour. Dick really got into it, saying, for instance, that in ULCA, they were taught to throw mud at signs saying "The Lutheran Hour," making a lot of facetious remarks about what a fine man Dr. Maier is, concluding with "But I never heard him," all in his best Jerry Lewis style. After about twenty minutes of this, Walt told us that Paul was Dr. Maier's son! I don't know when I have seen anything funnier. It's obvious that Dick really did think Dr. Maier was a fine man and that he was merely being funny, so we could find the tremendous blow it gave Dick more funny than it was damaging, but it all led to much laughter and comments about how Dick had just set Lutheran unity back by twenty years! Everyone got rather hilarious; Dick continuing to imitate Jerry Lewis perfectly. No doubt everyone thought we were drunk, and remarks as we left confirmed our suspicions that we were being objectionable to the people in the room not in on our fun—which was too bad in view of the fact that we had earlier made it known that we were Christians. As I write now, there is a party going on outside our door and they are being objectionable, but no one probably knows who they are or what they stand for. It doesn't help to feel bad about it now, though, since we know that *we* really enjoyed ourselves, regardless of what we might have been doing to others.

June 15, Midnight:

Quiet day. I slept quite a bit. It's still grey out. We feel we are becoming quite well acquainted as a group—beginning to know how people in general react to things. Jane and Bonnie are quiet but doing some serious, sound thinking; Paul is a good thinker, but enjoys life; Charlie is a bit quick, but comes up with brilliant statements . . . likes to get details straight; Phil seems somewhat placid, hates to hear us get steamed up about little things, wishes we would stick to discussing facts instead of trying to insert so many opinions; Marge, the redhead, seems impetuous, sincere, straight-thinking; Margaret Petrea says she is a "bit overwhelmed by everything and everyone." What an interesting group . . . and these are just some of them. I am impressed with how differently everyone interprets things that are said. The problem of real communication shows up in a group where everyone has a different background and each has definite ideas.

June 18, 1 A.M.:

What a life! No time to sleep. This trip was supposed to be very relaxing, but with a group this size, it seems no one wants to miss anything and something is always doing. What with 3 sessions a day and all the unplanned activities, we are busy all the time. I had good intentions of getting to bed at a reasonable hour tonight so I came back here before anyone else. I had only made a start at getting ready for bed when Barbara and Mary came in talking about the lights from land, so I put on my coat and a kerchief and went up to watch. It was 1½ hours later when I got back. It was a quieter day. Saw three or four beams

It was a special "Student Sailing" and this is what the deck looked like during free time.

from a school of fishing boats to one side of us. Three of us also watched the sunset, our first at sea because we usually have Bible study at that hour. The clouds have been interesting all day. The waves weren't particularly big but the swells were, and it felt as if someone had dropped my bed into space every little while last night. Tonight was the captain's dinner. I've *never* had so much to eat in a week. Each time we eat, I feel as if I would never eat again. The sky reminded me of the Chicago planetarium tonight because the stars were so bright. Beverly gave us an astronomy lesson. We also went to a lecture on existentialism in literature tonight, given by a Swarthmore College teacher who has been teaching French on the boat.

June 19, 1:20 A.M.:

Late again! Getting to bed is awfully difficult on this boat or with this group. Only two of us are in bed so far. We are docked at Le Havre, waiting to leave. We have been here since about 10:30 P.M. Barbara and I got up at 7:15 A.M. to eat breakfast. We were approaching the Isle of Wight with the sun shining on its white cliffs and hundreds of white sea gulls flying around the boat. We were thrilled! We spent a good part of the morning just watching the scenery. We got to Portsmouth about 1:30 P.M. There, the boat anchored and a smaller boat from Southampton came to get the Southampton passengers. The green fields and trees framed by hedges along the hillsides on shore and the red rays of the sun all made such beautiful scenery. There was much activity in the harbor with boats, planes, and luggage being transferred. A pilot of the small boat shouted directions for missing "Me mast" in his homey dialect. Our boys had shorts on and one woman looked at Dick and said, "There's one of those d—— silly Americans." We began to watch the coast of France about 9 P.M. and arrived at Le Havre about 10:30. It was still a little light when a pilot-boat came to meet us. That boat let down a smaller motorboat which came to our side and its pilot climbed up a rope ladder onto our boat. It all reminded me of some movie I might have seen. As we docked, there were big hoists, passageways rolling up to the boat, Frenchmen running around shouting in their strange language, bikes wheeling around on the dock below us. Foreign movies are becoming alive from this side of the ocean. Rotterdam, Amsterdam, Copenhagen—places we haven't even seen yet, but the names already *sound* different.

News from East Berlin has been changing every day.

A large number of passes for travel into West Berlin were to be issued and other concessions made. Yesterday, however, thousands rioted and demonstrated against the Soviet government and the city is now in a state of emergency. It's now 1:40 and we're on our way again. Another short night.

June 19, 3 P.M.:

I awakened feeling more rested than any other morning, probably because it was 10 A.M. before any of us even stirred. So many of the passengers are gone. We had the lounge to ourselves last night and we see no one else in the corridor this morning. It's grey outside and no scenery yet, so we've had a nice, lazy day—*at last*! It would have been quite a different trip if every day had been like this. More restful but perhaps boring after a while and less profitable for the future.

June 20, 1:30 A.M.:

Here we are in a lovely, rather quaint hotel in Amsterdam! The boat started down the Maas River about 4:30 P.M. and docked about 6 P.M. It's the strangest feeling to be a foreigner—to have money in your hands that you don't know how to use, to have a ticket you can't read. The Dutch all seem to speak English well, so it shouldn't be hard to get around, but one certainly does feel at a disadvantage. Holland seems so clean and precise, as if every flower and tree had been very deliberately placed, for a picture perhaps. Suppose with all the water around, there's never any dust for one thing? We took the train from Rotterdam to Amsterdam. Jane met a fellow who showed us what streetcar to take to our hotel, so all twenty of us piled on with all our luggage. I think the poor conductor was quite overcome! They served us a delicious dinner, including strawberries and whipped cream in their delightful little dining room when we arrived about 11 P.M.—our third big meal today! Three of us girls walked the streets afterwards but decided it was a mistake because everyone was *too* friendly. One fellow in a car stopped to try to get our attention; he said it was plain that we had come "from a distance," guessed we were Americans.

June 22, 1:30 A.M.:

These hours! This is our night to go to bed early and get lots of sleep! We rode train all day Saturday. Saw some wonderful sights and spent most of the day standing looking out the windows. We rode 4th class but it was very comfortable; I liked the arrangement of the train . . . privacy, a place to stand and look, less noise from the rest of the train. We met some interesting people during the day. The most beautiful sight was a high bridge over the Kiel Canal near Runesburg, Germany. The train went around in a complete circle to go over it and then under it. We were so high and the whole town with its red roofs and green gardens were spread out below us. I can't remember when I have seen anything more beautiful! We saw many other impressive sights as we passed through three countries. Humorous items: our train went very close to poles and tunnels so we ducked away from open windows frequently. We were told the joke about a man not understanding and taking it literally when told to "Look out!," so stuck his head out, to his sorrow. As we stopped at one station, we tried to see what town it was. Someone read "Herren" aloud, to the great amusement of a German couple we were riding with, since the sign meant "Gentleman's toilet." We arrived in Copenhagen one-and one-half-hours late. We were met by students carrying a large balloon face with a student cap on top, and we were then taken to a hostel to sleep. It was crowded, so we slept on dirty straw mats on the floor. The sheets were clean, thank goodness, but the blankets were filthy. We were too sleepy by 3:30 A.M. to notice much, however. As we went across the court, which was alive with Norwegian students celebrating final exams being over with a vacation, we remarked about how light it was for the hour. A bit later, we could read without difficulty. An unreal experience! We were warned the nearest W.C. (water closet) was being used by both men and women. Beverly and I went in together and found it filthy. She went into a stall and slammed the door. When she tried to open it and couldn't, she asked me to try, but I discovered there was no handle on the outside! So, at 2:30 A.M., Beverly was stuck in a toilet with no room to crawl out above or below. It struck us as very funny. A Norwegian boy came in and I told him what was going on. He went for help, came back and carried on a conversation with me in that filthy place until someone rescued Beverly.

Later in the day, we went to a communion service at Our Saviour's Cathedral nearby, the largest in Copenhagen. There were few people there but the choir and singing were good and the communion service impressive. Afterward, we climbed the 400 steps up to the top of the tower, the second highest point in the city. The stairs were on the outside toward the top so both the climb and the view were breathtaking. We took a ferry-boat most of

The Kofoeds Skole was our headquarters in Copenhagen, our first stay.

the way to a YMCA for a cheap but good dinner. These Danish openfaced sandwiches hit the spot. Next, we toured a Deaconess Hospital and Home (St. Luke's), where there are about 250 deaconesses. I have never seen such a clean place. They had a perfectly beautiful nursery where each nurse *lived* with four babies apiece. It looked ideal and I wanted to come back and learn more about it if I could. We were served coffee, cakes, and cookies before we left, during which we mainly talked with the students studying there. They spoke English well so we were able to talk about anything with them.

Margaret Petrea had friends who had been in Copenhagen and gotten acquainted with the Sihms. They looked her up after church this morning after having found out our complete schedule and making plans accordingly. They invited her and one other friend (I was lucky enough to be it) for supper. They picked us up at 5:00 in a car rented for the occasion and took us to Elsinore to see Krönberg Castle (Hamlet), Fredricksborg Castle and Hilleröd, and other places along the way. We got back to their lovely, gracious "flat," at 9:30, where we were served gin, vermouth, and a Danish meal of openfaced sandwiches—one with herring and onions, one with their small shrimp and liver sausage and cucumber. I passed up some small sandwich-size beef-steaks. The bread was buttered on a special board, the liver sausage loaf had "hello" written across it with fat; the shrimp and lettuce were placed on special small dishes at our place; some garnish was growing in soil in a rectangular dish with a special scissor to cut it, and American flags standing around in it! Schnapps was at each place in an individual *klok glas,* which says "klok, klok, klok" when you turn it over. Before we ate, the little girl, Helga, four years old, presented us each with some paper napkins that had Danish insignias and pictures. The conversation, manners, and numerous small acts of consideration made it the most marvelous entertainment I can conceive of—and toward perfect strangers to them, really! I believe in Danish hospitality. The other kids who had also eaten in and been entertained in private homes came back with almost as unbelievable stories. It's now 2:30 A.M. and getting light, so I guess anything else will just have to be forgotten.

This is a picture of our group in a relaxed study. I guess partly because everyone looked so relaxed and cheerful, I carried this in my billfold ever since.

June 22, 11 P.M.:

Today we saw Copenhagen on foot! We saw: 1) Statue of King Christian IV and buildings around designed by him 400 years ago. 2) Statue of nude figures given to Denmark by Norway for her help during the war—*Norje tokka Danske.* 3) The Little Mermaid, symbol of Hans Christian Anderson's fairy tale. 4) Statue of Victory near harbor. 5) Vessel in harbor commemorating sinking of their own ships when the Germans came; one ship left to block entrance. 6) Statue of Garfion, daughter of a king of Sweden. Legend is that she asked for a country of her own

31

to rule, that her father told her she could have what she could plow, so she cut out a piece of ground, she and her father threw it into the sea and it came up and became the Island of Zealand. 7) Statue of Christian on his famous horse in the middle of a circle of four palaces, almost alike. 8) Marble Church—was supposed to be built of marble but wasn't—is next to palaces, blue light from a window back of the altar, a sign outside meaning "His Word abideth forever"; planned at same time as palaces but not enough money. Half was built 100 years later and left; trees began to grow inside; completed 75 years ago. 9) Tower of *Folkes Kirche*. 10) Students in the street celebrating completion of exams; danced around statue of Frederick IV and saluted him. 11) Parliament building exterior only. New Constitution just passed—may now have a queen instead of a king; Greenland to be a part of Denmark instead of a colony; may give part of their sovereignty to union of Europe as NATO. 12) Fish women in fish market. 13) Statue of Absalom, founder of Copenhagen. 14) Parliament church where services held at opening of Parliament and for state funerals. 15) Parliament Supreme Court. 16) Cathedral Church with statues of 12 apostles by Thorwalden. Pulpit on side of church, benches facing it in aisle, two balconies, special throne seat on second balcony for king and queen. 17) Lunch at Skandia, made by our hosts; United States flag out on table; music throughout meal—delicious, juicy steak entrée. 18) Had discussion and lecture on Danish church by a Sociology professor at student headquarters, and "picnic" supper there of 4 smörbröd sandwiches. 19) Evening at Tivoli, the famous amusement park; symphony orchestra, pantomime stage, numerous other attractions. Fabulous place!

These nights in a hostel can really be something! The first night on the floor, the next two in a lower bunk with straw raining down on me every time Margaret, above me, turned or moved; then they put paper under the mattress and every time she moved a muscle, it crackled—no one was ever as restless as she seemed; group of girls in the room got up at 4:30, 3 hours after we had gone to bed, and took till 6:00 to clear out, very noisy the whole time. Last night, there must have been about 25 young English teenagers staying in the room; never heard so much chattering and noise. I did go to sleep about 1 A.M. with it going strong, still going on when I woke about 8 A.M. Wonder if we'll have any undisturbed rest this summer.

Tuesday, we took a bus trip to visit the Inner Mission "Mecca" of Denmark. We stopped to see a very old village church. At Haslev, we saw some of the unique Danish "folke schools." (More about them in notes elsewhere.) We also saw a huge old castle with acres and acres of beautiful grounds which one of the Danish students said he had never heard of anyone but personal friends of the count living there getting into, but he let us see some of it. We could see him wanting to let us in, but mentally debating about how far to let us go. First, he said, "I can show you the stables." Then "You can see the courtyard." Then, "I can't let people inside because if one comes in I have to let others in, but I will show you a couple of rooms." He showed us his china collection which he said is one of the largest in the world and it was fabulous! Everything we saw glittered and shone or was deep and rich looking—artistic, beautiful and uncluttered displays. We all automatically "oh'ed" and "ah'ed." The name of the place was Giselfeldt. In the evening, we had a campfire with the

Danish students at the site of the camp they themselves are building. Most of them biked the 15 miles or so out there, and had to go back yet at 12 midnight, when we broke up. We feel as if things are awfully lopsided most of the time. They speak our language, sing our songs, and we don't always have much to contribute. We must look as though we *expected* them to come our way, and they have really been putting themselves out. We feel deeply indebted to them and incapable of showing it adequately.

Yesterday, we toured churches of the "Church Fund" of Copenhagen. Their aim is to have smaller churches so the pastor can contact the people. They don't get the churches from the government, are raising money to build by themselves. In the afternoon, we saw Rosenborgade Castle. I was most surprised by the jeweled crowns and other royal gems. After that, we had some free time. In the evening, we had a discussion with the Danish students on various problems.

Am writing later, trying to think back. The students we meet seem to be doing a good deal of thinking. Our discussions got a little hot and out of hand at times and we were concerned. (*More in separate discussion notes.*) Thursday, we saw a film on Kofoers School, the hostel where we are staying, and took a bus tour into the country to see their training school. It is designed to restore self-respect or rehabilitate men who are just falling into crime and hopelessness. We got back just in time to dress up and go to Student Headquarters for strawberries and cream. Then we listened to a lecture by Kai Eric Lindquist on the student movement in Denmark. Everyone was tired and the discussion was slower than usual. Supper at the university cafeteria, then a breathing spell before we went to Gertrude and Anna Marie Peterson's lovely home for a garden party. The highlight of the eve-

ning for me was a long talk with Moses, a fellow who gave
a talk at the campfire about the importance of understanding oneself in the light of what one has been—in the
light of history and circumstances. It was deep and
thoughtful. He is a theological student, has half a year
left. He gave me a better understanding of Danish
church-life than anything else I had heard. He said there
was no such thing as a Danish church—that there were
many different movements, that each pastor had a great
deal of freedom to express his own views. Pastors are educated in the theology department of the University, then
apply to the bishop where they want to serve. The bishop
doesn't ask many questions about theology because he
knows they know more than he does and he doesn't want
to get involved. It seems to me that this system would cre-
ate a great deal of inconsistency, freedom, and disorgani-
zation within a rigid state setup. Moses did not want to
dispense with the theological training in the University.
He thought it was good to work out one's own faith in a
secular environment because it would be more thorough
than if theology was presented in a pious environment.
However, he did think pastors should have some short
training under the church before going to the ministry.
He thinks the spiritual conditions in Denmark are desperate and that movements such as the Church Fund are
okay, but far too superficial to cure the underlying problems. He says many want to see the church as it is col-
lapse. He thinks something will happen; he doesn't know
what and says many feel as he does but there has been no
opportunity for this feeling to break through yet. He
thinks the preacher must lead his people by his preaching
of the Word in a really challenging way to wake them and
help them grow up to the point of being able to criticize
themselves and make changes. Then, whatever happens

35

to the external setup will be in God's hands. It was most interesting and inspiring to meet such an earnest, keen-minded theological student. He goes with Lisa, a girl who also seems to have a very keen mind, a p.k. (preacher's kid) who read poetry at the campfire in the most beautiful voice. The fellow next to me said she just loves poetry, and her voice simply caressed the words. The evening in the garden was spent eating, talking, playing games and doing folk dances. My high heels didn't help me enjoy the latter, however. Dick P. and I got away early (11:30) and came home. We were all dead tired and had hoped to get some rest before we left Denmark.

June 26:

We got up and took our suitcases to the station, then Beverly and I went shopping until noon. We left for Oslo at 1 P.M. in the train. Until then, the weather had been very unusually bright, they told us. They thought it was very hot but we weren't uncomfortable. Paul and I sat together all the way, with the seats across taken by Bev, Ralph, and Dick at various times. Paul, Ralph and I had an extended discussion of education systems, and later Bev joined us for one about drama and other literature. I was so tired I felt almost ill when we got off the train. Letters from Armour and home involved problems which added stress. We were met at the train by a group of Norwegians. One of the Lager leaders was Dr. Flattorp. He asked me if he hadn't seen me before and we discovered that he just came back from America where he had taught my sisters Rhoda and Faith in his classes at Augsburg! I was put in the new Chevrolet (had seen few cars in Copenhagen) and taken to a very nice home, the Amundsens. We were *so* glad to hear we would be in quiet, peaceful homes!

June 27:

I woke during the night drenched in perspiration under the covering, a comforter enclosed in linen. It was all that was available for covering; too warm with it and too chilly without it. I only noticed there was a wash basin in the room when Inga Brit brought in a pail of hot water in the morning.

June 28:

We left on a two-day trip to Telemark. We spent the night in a lovely little village in a folke school building which was so new and neat and clean-looking. The mountain air was wonderful, and it was the most peaceful night's sleep since leaving America; even had a hot shower! Still it was 12:30 before I got a couple of letters written, so still no eight hours of sleep.

June 29:

We rode the bus till 6 P.M., outside of a visit and matins at a church and a few stops for lunch. We spent the eve at the Lager house with students from both student groups, but we were awfully tired and dirty.

June 30:

Another full day. We went to services at a large hospital, to a lecture, had a quick shopping trip, made a visit to the Folke Museum, spent the evening with young people at Fredricksborg parish house. Home at 12 midnight, washed my hair after that. This lack of sleep and the fast pace is really wearing. I don't see how we can keep it up all summer.

July 1:

Our schedule was less hectic today in spite of three lectures and a discussion; not much of the latter today. We were all tired. The weather has been hotter than for 50 years, the papers say—all the time we've been here, which doesn't help. They say the temp. is usually about 20° C and has now been 30° C. We shopped this afternoon, and then I came back to Amundsens to spend two–three hours with my hostesses for a change. The folks are on vacation so Inga Brit and Anita have entertained me. Inga Brit is a member of the Laget group; a warm, gracious, open person with a natural sort of piety. She plays the piano well and studies language. Anita seems rebellious in a subtle way, though very intelligent, I'm sure. She is very considerate of my wants, added flowers to my room. They have an older sister who was in Salzburg, Germany at a work camp three years ago, before going to Hannover last year. She is now a medical student. They brought out an album of hers to show me, and I discovered that my nursing classmate, Virginia Jackson, and an Augie classmate, Marian Lack, were at the same work camp!

I didn't get to say good-bye to Dr. Flattorp; haven't

seen him since last Monday. Rev. Svein-Hanson has made a growing impression on us. The Laget seems to me to have a more healthy attitude than the pietists, from what we have seen of them. Rev. Svein says the Oxford Movement has influenced their work, has restored a lost emphasis on confession, and they believe in small discussion groups whose members are free to discuss everything that presents a problem to them in a personal way. He says Oxford people had a saying that you could not be used fully until there was nothing in your life which you could not discuss or admit to another person, that confession and fellowship was necessary for full growth and experience in Christianity. It seems to me it agrees with psychiatric principles as well as the Christian principle that we must learn to accept others as they are as God has accepted us. Again, it will be midnight before I turn out the light! Will I ever get eight hours of sleep again? I'm glad to get this caught up, however.

July 2:

This is Crown Prince Olav's 50th birthday. Everyone wore little pins, flags all out. We left on the 9 A.M. train. A kind Norwegian boy volunteered to carry my suitcase shortly after I got off the bus, for which I was very thankful since it was several blocks to the station. It has been some advantage to have had one heavy suitcase because our hosts have often volunteered to carry it—to the point that I have been uncomfortable about it at times. This Norwegian spoke to me in Norwegian, which pleased me; I like to be taken for one when I'm in Norway. We continued the conversation in English, however. Most of us slept off and on all the way to Stockholm, which was good

What I like about this picture is Dr. Stendhal looking very much a part of us, which he was. He is probably seeing us off from Sweden.

since we were all suffering from lack of sleep. I've never seen the group so quiet. We are told there is a paratyphus epidemic in Sweden—30 dead and 2500 ill, which scared us into resting too, I think. (*I have specific memories of seeing sights in Oslo and also in the countryside, but I don't know when we found the time for sight-seeing, and guess I was too tired to do as thorough a job of recording events as usual.*)

We arrived in Stockholm on schedule about 6:10 P.M. And there was Rev. Stendahl waiting for us. He had made such an impression on me last year when he visited Chicago. We were taken to the hostel and given one-half-hour to clean up, change clothes, and be on our way to Skansen by ferry. There is a *Tivoli*-type amusement park and mid-way, plus a very high-class restaurant. Our boys had not cleaned up and we were told they would not have let us in if we hadn't been Americans, which made us cringe. We stayed there until 10:30 eating in leisurely fashion, a wonderfully relaxing way to spend the eve. We could look over most of the city after having gone up the highest escalator I have been on to get there. A Swedish girl, Ingalla, sat at our table. She came out with some surprising comments, such as when I asked her if the spinach went beside the potatoes—since in Denmark, it had gone over them—she said, "You can try the tablecloth or your glass. We usually use the plate." She was very attractive and was pretty formal-looking, so we were not prepared for her remarks. She said Swedes are self-conscious in trying to make an impression and that might result in such comments—her idea of trying to be entertaining. We had to be in at 11:30 so we gladly came back and were actually all in bed on our unpredictably shaped mattresses by 12:15.

Wonderful!

July 3:

We spent the day getting on board and sailing to Finland. The Swedish ship was very nice and it was great to spend a day just eating and sleeping. We did have a session on Norway and there were a few irritable reactions afterwards. Paul, Bev, and I talked in our cabin until suppertime; afterwards Bev and I wrote letters and went to bed. We didn't fall asleep right away in spite of the soft mattresses, so Bev and I got up about 12:30 to see what the moon and water looked like on a light night.

July 4:

We arrived in Helsinki at 9 P.M. and were met by Rev. Juva. We got settled in a hostel, went to the post office and bank, did some sightseeing. We visited St. Nicholas, the great church since independence, with the University buildings below. We saw the National Art Museum paintings and sculptures, ate lunch—deciding living standards were not high here—made a quick but profitable trip with a guide, through the Historical Museum, where we saw some very unique things from Finland's past. The most notable thing was the difference in colors of things made in East and West Finland. In the West, (West Finland used to belong to Sweden) there were Swedish colors, which are bright, but in the east, they used what our guide called "true" Finnish colors—somber, smoky shades of blue, yellow, brown and green. Then, we went to the Olympic stadium. We laughed at the way Mardy was literally jammed into the elevator by the man in charge to get us to the tower. After lunch, we dressed in our best to go to a "reception" in honor of the Fourth of July by the consul at the American legation. It turned out to be more of a picnic. Mrs. Seyda and Barbara D. won champagne and liquor bottles for winning a guessing game. We found that funny and promised to include that in our reports on the trip. From there we went to the SCM (Student Christian Movement) rooms for a meeting with students. There was a lot of mixing and conversation and I think it was a successful evening. We are the first large group of Lutherans to ever officially visit Finland, and both they and we are excited about that. Their art and the things they say about themselves, as well as their achievement record, indicate that they are a somewhat melancholy people who have suffered a great deal, who have had to struggle hard for everything they get, but who have hope and courage. We are amazed at the modern new buildings everywhere. They would seem to indicate prosperity, but in view of their poor living standards, inflation, their need to repay WWII loans, and other financial feats, it indicates independence, self-sacrifice, and discipline instead.

July 5:

We spent a most enjoyable day at Tuusula parish, attended services and then spent the afternoon until 8 P.M.at the Parish Institute. We had lectures and discussions but we had time in between to relax, go down to the lake, and enjoy ourselves. It is such a lovely place. It was built mostly with U.S. National Lutheran Council section of the LWF. We got back early in the eve, which made it still more relaxing and enjoyable.

I find myself thinking that all the things transplanted to America by foreigners, such as buildings, their religion, just aren't the same when they are transplanted. It makes me see that it is important to be oneself in one's particular circumstances, developing as the situation requires. I will appreciate the American part of America more for seeing that the things transplanted from other cultures look so much better in their original settings.

I had a talk with a Finnish boy today about communism, McCarthyism, and more. He says that every communist knows that America has concentration camps ready for communists in case of war, due to McCarthy's efforts mainly, I take it.

Beds: the one here is boards with a thin mattress—comfortable at that—but there are about fifty people on this floor, boys and girls, to use one washroom with two sinks and a toilet. Are we having fun trying to wash clothes and hair, besides just trying to wash faces and brush teeth. I just took my first cold-water shampoo.

July 6:

Annali came at 9:30 to take us downtown briefly, then out to the College of Nursing. It is a beautiful, very modern building. All this birch woodwork adds a lot too. There are 600 students there. Her aunt is the director of the College, her father a doctor there, and her brother is her boss in the Public Health Department. She was so shy when she first met us that she could scarcely whisper, but she was very self-assured in the hospital and has become different around us too, gradually. I can imagine how overcome she might have been at first, meeting such a large group of Americans for the first time. After lunch, we had a discussion on social responsibilities of the church, which started a great deal of discussion between the Finns and us and between members of our group. Phil, who is our quietest—or professes to be—, Mary, Charles, Paul and I had quite a discussion afterwards. Most everyone in the group took part in the discussion for a change. I've noticed a change in that respect; I hope it isn't just temporary; Peg and others are mixing much more than at first and taking an active part. The cliques have been the same all along, but there is more mixing as well.

In the late afternoon, we visited the dormitories out in the country, for the Technical University. I can't get over the beautiful modern buildings. We were supposed to have a discussion but it got a little late so Mr. Lehtonen suggested we just look instead. We also stopped for a few minutes to see the War Memorial in Helsinki. I shed a few tears telling Mardy about brother Paul's grave. We spent more time seeing a typical Finnish home, typical of the educated people probably, because it was full of art and handwork; very attractive. I think their wicker furniture, the birchwood furniture, the scarfs, rugs, pillows, wall hangings are all beautiful. I was ready to go home, get married, and start fixing up a home. We got back just in time to pack our last minute things in our suitcases and catch the train. We had berths, three to a compartment. They were third class but nice and had water basins. The beds were rather hard and it was chilly enough that I put on my sweater and spread my coat on top of me.

July 7:

We arrived at Punkasalim [*haven't found on maps or itinerary but that is the way I had spelled it in my diary*] at 11 A.M. The people in the other car discovered it was our stop as they were in the middle of card games, brushing teeth and what not; they piled out in a mighty big hurry with confusion on the part of all. It was quite funny. We had a big breakfast when we arrived at Camp Teinharju. It was built with American Lutheran Student Association funds, which the Finnish students used to buy and sell coffee, increasing the money a great deal. There is no running water, but it is a beautiful place, has as attractive cabins as any camp I've seen, and the scenery is great! Lehtonens told us we would have the day to relax. These Finns apparently think rest and relaxation are important, judging by the way they have entertained us and that has been wonderful! We had breakfast at 10:30, explored until 1:30, had coffee, then a sauna, and what an experience that was! Never felt cleaner and we all really needed it. One feels as though one can't breathe when the steam first hits, but then it gets comfortable and the perspiration rolls, really cleaning out the pores, I'm sure. The Finnish girl with us said it was about 70–80 C. We steamed for a while, plunged into the lake in the nude. It's cold out today so that was cause for much screaming but wasn't as bad as we had expected. We went back into the steam for a bit, washed, then back to the steam, then took another plunge. It left a real tingle! We loved it and we are all ready for another one tomorrow. I think they were all pleased that we liked it. (There was some squeamishness about possibility of the boys being close enough to see us girls in the water and vice versa.) We washed a few clothes in the lake afterwards.

Tonight we had a discussion on evangelism in the University with Rev. Seyda leading. The two Finnish secretaries were the only ones who contributed though; it was translated for us by one of their group. Seyda talked about problems of the situation; the Finns wanted to know what the *content* of the *message* should be. We discussed organization; they wanted to know what kind of a witness the group could make as a community of saved sinners which individuals could not make. It was so obvious that they were frustrated because the discussion didn't get deep enough. I tried to get it deeper too, because I felt so strongly that it needed to, but Seyda ended up saying the discussion illustrated our differences in thinking because of our situation; that it was to be expected—which I thought was completely untrue and only erected a false barrier. Mr. Lehtonen added that he felt it was a generalization to think that they were always concerned about community witness because they were just starting to think of it in their Student Christian Movement (SCM). I don't see how a sense of forgiveness of sin can help but result in a sense of community and assumptions of our fellowman which are unique, though I confess that many things burden this realization in my own life. I do believe with all my heart that it is central to our approach in "evangelizing" others to accept them as Christ has accepted them. We gathered around the fireplace, and sang for a long time, had devotions, took a walk around the lake. I'm going to hate to leave this place!

Miscellaneous: the pots in drawers on the train; a small little train whistle that sounded like a toy whistle; trains and buses going over the same bridges; no longer Damen and Herren, but Naiset and Miehet; Ralph having sent his bus ticket home to Dick's place in Kansas with other things; Dick falling in the creek while washing clothes; beard growing now the subject of conversation.

July 8:

Last night, we took a walk around the lake at 11:30 P.M. It was so light that I took a picture, don't know whether it will turn out or not. We could see our way perfectly, more like what we would have expected hours later. We looked at the hugo stones that the Finns had set up to serve as a defense if the Russians came across the lake because they were very close to them. It all looked so ominous and desperate, especially in the half-light because it made the stones whiter, starker. There were also some trenches or pits of some kind dug out too. It brought the war much closer to us than before seeing these markers in such now peaceful surroundings.

We began this morning with matins, breakfast, and Bible study on Jonah. I was rather furious with Rev.

Seyda, who was leading our group, because when I tried to get away from a discussion of whether or not God could reveal His will through lots by saying I thought the important thing was that it created the necessary sense of responsibility in such an instance, he didn't even try to understand. However, the group did. Rev. Seyda said, "Well, maybe your mentality will allow you to think that way, but I think . . ." I clarified my point to him later and he apologized, but I object to his readiness to attribute ideas that aren't naturally his own to some strange or foreign type of mentality. He has done that quite often. Some of the group are considering going to talk to him rather than talk behind his back. I don't know what would help. Maybe his attitude isn't so important, but it does frustrate others. Tonight, we had a discussion of the ecumenical problems in the University led by the Finns. As usual, I felt that they were trying to go deeper and our leader kept it superficial. I sat there wondering if there was nothing he felt he needed to go deeper into or learn more about, or if he considers this trip purely to exchange information. I don't dislike him but I do regret his attitude and way of thinking and find it frustrating.

After a quick lunch, we took a bus trip to Savonlinna to see an 800-year-old castle, built at the Finnish-Russian angle at the time. We really went through it and found it quite fascinating. It reeked with atmosphere; had been a former prison where dead bodies were allowed to accumulate in a pit where the worst criminals were dropped. This went on for 200 years. We sang most of the way on the trip. We got back in time for another delightful sauna. After supper, we had our discussion and left; the cart and horse again taking our luggage and we hiking. We had lumps in our throats as we waved good bye and hated to leave; more so than leaving other places so far. We were able to relax and they made us feel such a part of things, not at all like visitors to be taken about and shown everything. There is also something so simple and natural about them that I think one just naturally drops any pose too; they put us off guard. We passed the Russian border a bit ago. The train looks the same as the last one except that the bunks seem just a bit softer.

July 9:

En route, the S.S. *Williams* to Stockholm from Turku. We only had a five-minute leeway between trains in Helsinki and it became obvious that we wouldn't make it, so a Finnish man who had been talking to some of the group suggested we get off at 6:30 A.M. and take a northern route to Turku. We did and made it to Turku two hours early, but were disappointed at not going through the Russian zone because we were told the shades would be pulled down and engines changed for that stretch. I got a big smile from a little Finnish girl for a package of gum as I left. I had tried to talk to her daddy last night. He didn't know any English but managed by knowing some words like daddy, Chicago, St. Petersburg, April, to let me know his aunt lived in St. Petersburg and his uncle in Chicago and that his aunt was coming to Helsinki in August. He made motions on his hand from a point that was St. Petersburg to a point he named Helsinki, etc. Risto Lehtonen was pleased, I think, to show us around Turku all afternoon, since that is his home, but I felt sorry for him as he pointed out his home as we passed, but had to go on with us for the afternoon instead of stopping there after a hard week. He must be very tired! I don't think I'll ever forget his boyish face, his bright blue eyes matching his slightly deeper blue jacket of a pretty shade seen quite often over here; also his bow tie and the surprisingly deep and mature thinking that he expressed with an eager shine in his eyes. Perhaps he was one thing that touched our hearts. As I mentioned in letters I was writing last night, I wonder if those saunas wouldn't break down a lot of barriers between people in our own country if we had them. It's very hard for us to analyze the feelings we developed about the people we were with in Finland. We met some fine people this afternoon too, at the very modern youth home at Turku University, some very nice looking and alert students, also the director of the Church Rehab program.

This boat isn't quite as nice as the *Birger Jast* which took us to Helsinki, but it is comfortable and we've been having a very chummy evening making ourselves at home in the first-class cabin lounge with the stuffed chairs and writing tables and a piano. We've been talking over our trip and the general attitude seems to be that we feel strongly that it is what we do for and mean to the people we meet as friends that will influence their thinking towards America more than anything we can try to do or say to defend and justify American foreign policy, etc., though we do have numerous opportunities to informally correct misconceptions, explain, and interpret.

One of the difficulties of our travel in Scandinavia is predicting meals and menus. We have several times been almost starved by 11:30 to 1:00 P.M. when the first real meal arrives, which may be porridge, then we are stuffed with two hour feedings the rest of the day. We never know what to expect. In Skansen, we went easy on the salad and *brod* at the beginning and then during a long wait, the rumor went around that that had been our dinner and we were panicky for a bit until the main course arrived.

This noon, we gorged ourselves at 1:00 P.M. because we had had little before then; feeding on the smörbröd and potatoes which have often been our noon meal. When we were ready for dessert, the meat and potatoes arrived! It was most embarrassing and funny, especially because we had fought over the last piece of cheese for our *smörbröd*. This noon, a piece of *knäckebröd* on my bread and butter plate was one of the few pieces of food left at our section of the table when Mary reached around an empty platter and helped herself to it, saying, "Excuse me," thinking it was a serving plate. It was so unconscious that it set me off.

On the same order of difficulties was our going to Skansen with any old clothes and being admitted only because we were *American,* then dressing our best for the reception at the legation, which turned out to be more of a picnic around a campfire.

July 10:

I got up at 7 A.M., was supposed to lead devotions at 8:30, then have a discussion on Finland at 8:45 and get to Stockholm at 10 A.M., but somehow or other, we landed at 8 A.M. instead. We had devotions and our meeting at the hostel instead. I was quite thrilled because so many offered sentence prayers after my part, praying for awareness of, forgiveness for, and help in overcoming personal short-comings—a general atmosphere of humility and unity which I see as a big change since we started out. The meeting proceeded very smoothly with Rev. Seyda even accurately summing up the way everyone felt about the hardships—war history, etc.—of the Finns and their courage and favorable attitude towards America.

We spent the afternoon sightseeing and visiting with the Swedish students as guides. We did an unusual amount of chummy talking with members of their group, enjoyed them much. A few bits to remember: Ulf with his red hair and twinkling blue eyes—certainly not a typical Swede with his gay humor, rather the most American person we have met perhaps. Someone asked the Swedish girl at the Stadsmission if that was considered a poor section of town; she hesitated a moment and then answered, "The palace is nearby, of course." That seems typical of the Swedish humor we have encountered a number of times, having a tinge of contempt or sarcasm. Some of them seem very cynical about Americans. Today, we heard that all Americans want turkey and ice cream every day, that they all chew gum, drink cokes, smoke, and that we have women on all ads. It feels as though they don't quite believe we like them sometimes. Our evening at the King's Tower Pagod restaurant was very successful, however, with twelve of us. We also met a foursome who are going to a World Council of Churches ecumenical camp near here; a colored New Yorker, an Indian, a Berliner, and a Stockholm nurse who is going to Africa shortly. They all seemed like very dynamic people. We found out that *Hissi Hiss* means elevator in Finnish and Swedish. I've had fun with my Swedish here, finding a few words useful. It is fun to see people's faces light up sometimes when a couple of words of Swedish clarify the situation. But the other side of the picture: when I asked a waitress if they had any *brod* on ship, she gave back a long spiel in Swedish which I couldn't understand, asking Ulf something and having him tell me to warn him if I was going to talk in Swedish so he didn't just think he couldn't understand my English. And when I asked a waitress for a hard-boiled egg yesterday in Swedish, she asked me if I couldn't say it in English so she could understand.

July 11:

We spent the morning doing a bit of shopping, mostly at Hemslöyd, some at N.K. We could have spent days there. We left at 11:50 A.M. and arrived at Sigtuna at 1:30 or so. We had lunch and some opening sessions the rest of the day. I was very impressed with the afternoon address by Rev. Sorgny Bolin of Uppsala. I am anxious to meet more of the students here. They come from Sweden, Norway, Denmark, and Finland—a few of whom we have met before. In the eve, we had a session of telling students from the other countries what we thought of them and they of us. I thought their criticisms were more thoughtful and valid than ours of them on the whole, perhaps because most of them have had more exposure to Americans than we have had to the Scandinavians. Opinions in our group varied more than among them too, it seemed. Many of their criticisms added up to superficiality on our part—inability to criticize ourselves or accept others' criticism, over-optimism, broad interest in every little thing but hard to talk to about deep things. I think I have seen a great deal of it exemplified, but we in turn wish we could make some of them see the importance of doing something. One of them said a bit ago, "We spend so much time speculating; sometimes we wish you Americans would tell us to do something." It seems to me that the Swedes still have a way of making us look bad every time we open our mouths. It reminds me a bit of the way Aunt Caroline can be at times. It's partly human, partly humor, but it feels as though there is also hostility in it—maybe not to us but to life in general. Rev. Stendahl commented that the Swedes are nihilistic because they are reacting against, rather than creating anything. Though he also says that partly, they are just reacting against any kind of Phariseeism.

We like our hostel quarters here; beds are softer, water very cold, however. Sigtuna is a most picturesque and interesting town.

July 12:

We had communion services at chapel at 8:30 A.M. After breakfast, most of us went to the village services at Mariakirchen, which is the most beautiful old church I have seen. In the afternoon, Rev. Olov Hartmann, Director of the Sigtuna Foundation, talked about his play, *The Holy City,* or *Den Helige Stad,* which we will be seeing. It was a rare privilege to hear him. Our Bible study groups met for the first time. I didn't think we accomplished a great deal; we disagreed with some of the ideas, though they were stated so generally that it was hard to be sure of the points being made. In the eve, Dr. Bodensieck read a long paper which was a bit hard to follow, but we ended up with a marvelous discussion. I am again (was in Chicago) impressed with Dr. Stendahl's shrewd analysis in so many areas. He can be very caustic and I wonder if Rev. Seyda resents that, and if he minds not having much to contribute when Stendahl and some of the Scandinavians get started; on the whole we are glad to listen to them. (Ralph and I are on the steering committee, and last night when we met, I told Dr. Stendahl that we feel that the Swedes are always putting us down. Two minutes later, Dr. Stendahl did the very thing to me, and Ralph snorted for the next ten minutes!)

July 13:

Sessions during the day, at which we became more talkative and the discussions more fruitful. I'm afraid that Rev. Seyda, the one who is most concerned about the impression we are making, asking if we are contributing our full share or are being passed by, is making the worst impression (by trying too hard?). I hope in general, we are getting a lot out of the discussions. The Scandinavians in Marge M.'s group say she is very good and is seeing the important things.

In the eve, we saw Hartmann's play in the outdoor theater at Sigtuna Foundation. Since the play was written for the particular location, very few props were needed; it was very effective. I hope to find a copy of it [I found one later in the U.S.].

July 14:

Rueben Hummel, the grandson of Dad's cousin, Erik Eriksson and son of Elida Eriksson Hummel, who was a child growing up in the same household with Dad in Harmånger after his father went to America, showed up at noon looking for me. (Dad had sent Elida our schedule.) He roared up on a motorcycle with the long hair a lot of the Swedes wear, put out his hand and said, "I'm Rueben, your Swedish cousin." It was a strange feeling to meet a real Swede that I was actually related to. He is in engineer's training in Stockholm, will be taking me home to Tuna-Hästberg over the weekend. I liked him!

We continue to have what seem like rebuffs from the Scandinavians, but maybe it's just that it is an effort for them to always talk English because at other times, they seem friendly enough. One is alone with them and tries to start a conversation and they go on in their own language. Maybe we do that too? I know I talk fast, which makes it hard for them to understand.

I have received and worked out a lot of ideas in our discussion groups which I want to go deep in me. Many of them are in my notes on our sessions, but I don't have time to jot them all down and at times, the discussions are too intense to stop for notes.

Tonight we ended by singing some Negro spirituals. I really enjoy singing with our group. I am surprised at how interested they are in our Negro spirituals.

I am a bit embarrassed but not sorry at an incident during our discussion tonight: Rev. Seyda and Charlie were talking about how it is a problem in our country to get the big shots into our student groups, and the groups can get the reputation of being for weak characters only. I interrupted to say that we had mentioned in our discussion group that we evangelize because of the other person's need and not our own! That stopped the discussion dead; I would rather it hadn't, but remembering that could help us to examine our motivations.

July 15:

A very good day! I did get into an argument during our Bible study with Rev. Seyda, who was visiting our group. He doubted that a habitual drinker could be justified by faith; the Danish pastor took exception, saying that the drinker might have fought it all his life and due to some psychological weakness been unable or overcome. Rev. Seyda was not convinced and spent half an hour telling us how he had "cured" a man who couldn't get along with his wife by being a little stern with him. I admitted that "supportive" treatment might work sometimes, but that it also might not; that if we are to argue that a man can always cure himself of drunkenness, we must also suppose that we can cure ourselves of many less obvious sins which stick to us all our lives but don't happen to bother the next fellow as much as drunkenness, but which are still sin and perhaps worse sin before God, because the drunkard is less likely to pride himself on his spiritual condition. I wonder if I am not more intense because I feel that my brother John might not have suffered as he did if Dad had been less sure that everyone could be like himself and hadn't had such impossible standards.

I had some satisfying conversations with some of the Scandinavians whom I had thought were a bit snobbish. One of them put his arm around me and said something and when I answered, he said, "You talk so fast. I can't understand you." I guess that's why they seemed to prefer their own company at first. Today, I feel that a few more days together would really deepen our contacts and be most worthwhile. I think that a lot of barriers and prejudices have been broken down as is, between Americans and Scandinavians—I hope.

Ralph, Dick, and Ingalil asked me to have a snack

with them after the evening session. Dick had stopped to see Rev. Stendahl to confess the feelings he had towards Rev. Seyda, because he said he couldn't take communion in the A.M. feeling as he does. We talked mostly about that till 1:30 A.M., and I was so tired. Rev. Stendahl told him to talk to Rev. Seyda. I didn't tell him what to do, did tell him I didn't think Rev. Seyda was the sort who would hold any grudges so he needn't fear on that score. I don't think it would change Rev. Seyda but I think something needs to change. Dick and Mardy have been griping constantly and it isn't doing any good.

July 16:

I searched myself very hard before and during communion. Dick told me he had talked to Rev. Seyda beforehand, and I asked myself if I were really hostile to Rev. Seyda as a person. Am I sure that I *want* the rest to be objective and really get along with him, or am I being the big sister trying to fight battles against a misunderstanding parent again, even when I think my criticisms are objective? Anyone needs to be on guard against such hidden motives, and I'm not sure I am innocent of them. I don't want his ideas to prevail, but maybe I am being more intense about it than I realize or need to be.

We left Sigtuna at noon after throwing a few bouquets to each other. Ulf, who has been in my group in the morning and Marge M.'s in the afternoon, said the group had made a real impression, that he felt that he had had his ideas changed and had a new outlook on hope and the necessity of action because of the Americans' "activism" as he had seen it. Rev. Stendahl said that if we made an impression on Ulf, we had really made an impact. We are glad to know we might have left something because *we* certainly gained.

We spent the afternoon at Old Uppsala. Then, Rev. Stendahl invited us to cook supper at his home. He walked us home after a pleasant time, and stayed to talk to Bev, Carolyn G., and me about the group's reaction to Rev. Seyda, as a result of Dick's talk with him in part. Carolyn and I arc at the opposite ends of age, so it gave him a range of reactions. We came to some conclusions: talking to Rev. Seyda won't change him; we are over-estimating the damage he can do to the Europeans' opinion of our group, though we do need to be more active in discussions if he isn't going to dominate with his ideas; we need to keep our courage up when we don't succeed in handling him; we must not "gossip" or "gripe" about him since we all know his faults now, and too much talk only breaks down morale; part of the tension we feel comes from the close living under a situation which produces tensions; he may be a scapegoat for the group's tensions and as such be good for group unity—the group has been remarkably free of tensions within, the main division being between students and Rev. Seyda

We stayed at a hostel which is usually used as a residence for students and we all had lovely single rooms. Mine apparently belonged to an athlete who lifts dumb bells for exercise. Bev couldn't find her room when wo came in at 12:30 A.M. and we were half hysterical as wc went up and down stairs trying to decide where her room could be, trying her key in some doors without success. We finally discovered a door to another section where her own door was concealed.

July 17:

I couldn't get my door unlocked this morning; my key kept turning but nothing happened, so I had to go through the room next door where Frank was, and out through his door. The whole morning was very mixed up because everyone had so many plans to figure out before we parted at noon for optional travels for the next six days. Poor Lars, our guide, was quite distraught, I think, and I wondered if 20 isn't too many people to handle. I left the group with Dick and Ingalil at 10:30. Ing and Gertrude took me on a very fast shopping trip and then left me to find my own way to the hostel to meet Bev and get our train for Stockholm. I don't know why Ingalil is so nice to me. I didn't deserve anything from her.

It wasn't easy finding my way back to the hostel, or dealing with people in a bookstore where I stopped off, where no one talked any English, but I made it. Bev and I reached the train station in time to have a snack, had more on the train. Rev. Stendahl took the same train back to Stockholm with us. Rueben Hummel met us at the station, took us to the American Express where we picked up mail (letters from Armour for me) and money. Then, went to see the Carl Milles garden. It was so wonderful to have a guide and be free to look at what we wanted to look at without 20 other people looking at the same thing. I wasn't aware that I minded being part of a group until I found myself appreciating the difference. Rueben and I took the train to Ludvika at 6:30 P.M. and arrived at Tuna Hästberg and his home about 11:30. I like him very much; he is very considerate . . . sure of himself in a natural way and has a sense of humor. The whole family were waiting up with a big meal, so we ate and didn't get to bed till 2:00 A.M. Such a nice family and a very attractive home. Elida reminds me of Aunt Helen in looks, is a very calm and motherly person, however.

July 18:

I slept till 10:30 or so. I was puzzled to be asked if I wanted a cup of coffee, and when I hesitated, was told that Elida's sister Greta wasn't up yet and I might want to wait for her. I still don't understand the Scandinavian meal system. We ate every hour or two once we started. I didn't understand how there was time for them to do anything but prepare and clean up after the meals. The first thing I did was to pack up a box to send home. Rueben helped me, and then he took me and it on his bicycle to the Hästberg post office. We also looked at a Swedish steam bath (*bastu*) and a laundry at Hästberg. By the time we got back, it was 2 P.M. and time for our next meal—a big one. Then, I washed clothes. Barbro, the daughter of the family, and her new husband Lars, arrived in the meantime. We all went to a neighbor's house for coffee and a visit; I think Solberg was his name. He had numerous medals and trophies from shooting and skiing. They had a teenage D.P. (displaced person) boy with them whose hobby was baking, so we had some of his goodies. An 82-year-old man named Almquist arrived who had been in America several times and was very anxious to meet and talk with an American. I didn't have to talk much, however, because he had so much to tell about meeting the king and having his picture taken with him when the king visited the home where he stays. Then, it was time to go home and eat a little again, then take a boat ride to their uncle Gunnard Hummel's place across the lake. It was raining a little and neither Lars nor Sven Eric (younger brother of Rueben's) made much use of the English they supposedly know somewhat, but the lake was beautiful and I managed to talk with them a little. (Lars, Barbro, Sven Eric, and I in the boat; Rueben had excused himself earlier to meet a girl with whom he had a date.)

Gunnard's wife is a former teacher and had visited America, so she too was interested in talking English with me. We both talked half English and half Swedish. Gunnard tried too, but I couldn't understand him, and was sorry to disappoint him. Lars and Sven Eric tried hard not to laugh at us. I had thought Rueben was gone for the evening but he and his girlfriend were there when we got back to the house. She is going to be a teacher and knew some English also; she was calm, rosy-cheeked and modest, but alert and sharp, not at all clinging or seductive. She made a good impression on me. We all sat around the table after finishing the meal and worked at magic tricks and play, much as we often did during eves at home. They all seemed to enjoy each other's company—lots of laughter. Rueben teased Greta a lot. He says he has the best nature in the family. "I always win fair though," he said, and says Barbro has the hottest temper, which I can believe because she is so quick in her reactions. She has a very soft, almost cooing voice which I loved to listen to. We finally broke up about 12:30, though I stayed up to wash my hair and catch up with this diary from way back.

July 19:

I didn't wake up until 10:45 A.M. so church was out. I don't know how much it means to them. Rueben said his aunt Greta was Baptist and I have the idea she is quite devout. Mr. Hummel is, or was, according to a history of Dalarna which they showed me, on the State Church Board for the local parish. Rueben says he himself doesn't go to or belong to any church. We took Torsten's (third of the boys) car and went for a two hour ride around their part of Dalarna. There are high hills, evergreen trees, water, valleys everywhere. They say it is a part of Sweden that is very popular with tourists and I can see why. Hummels have a beautiful view from their home. They have neighbors living so close that I at first thought their home was one of the Hummel farm buildings. Hummels have flowers everywhere and a sun dial in their yard. It gave me a thrill to see their flag flying and to be told that it was up in honor of my visit—something they commonly do for visitors. Other interesting bits from our ride: the Maypoles with their Dalarna crests, the Grangarde church—especially the view from across the lake; the Russian spires on the churches; the lovely little villages with their red houses amidst the green trees. I would like to have had a picture of them but would have needed a wider view than I could capture on my camera. We climbed the *Klocken,* a high hill with a house where they store hay till winter and then bring it down on sleds. Rueben pointed out the place in the hills where the women take the cattle during the summer and make *mersmör* and other products from the milk. Speaking of *mersmör*, I have asked other Swedes if they were familiar with that or *tät mjölk,* both of which Mother makes, but they haven't known about them. But we have had both here, and it really makes me feel that this is where my roots are. I assume Mother learned to make them from Dad's sisters, or did Dad know how?

We returned to a big dinner about 3 P.M., topped by fresh strawberries and cream, which we have had frequently in Scandinavia. We have also had "clamberries" which look like blackberries in shape, but are reddish-yellow and transparent, unlike any berries I have seen. After dinner, all of us—including Eivon, Rueben's girlfriend who was there—went out and played badminton for a while, then went swimming at a nice beach; I wore Barbro's suit. After that, we visited another brother of Werner and Gunnar Hummel who lives at the same lake during the summer. We came back and ate again, played more badminton, ate again. Torsten and I went along to take Eivon home, stopping at Lake Malaren, one of the most beautiful, Rueben says, has many islands and coves.

Though I enjoyed this group so very much, I wished so that I knew Swedish better because I certainly missed out on a lot. They were so considerate that I didn't feel left out but conversation was limited by my sparse Swedish. Anita, a 13-year-old foster-child of Elida's brother who was visiting them (Elida had had a Finnish child staying with them during the war as many around them did) and Sven Eric had least to say to me, but even they had loosened up and were saying a few words to me in English by the time I left. I think Lars knew more than he used; they have only been married for a month; Barbro and I did pretty well. Greta, who is a thirty-one-year-old nurse, understood quite a bit but couldn't say much. Torsten and Mr. Hummel seemed to know little. I went ahead and tried to communicate with all, Swedish at various times, but it was pretty slow and I knew how painfully "broken" it must have sounded. I suspected Rueben, especially, was controlling his mirth at times. But I was glad for the little I did know.

July 20:

We were up at 5 A.M. and off at 6:10 A.M.. Elida and Anita took the train to the next stop, then changed for a train to take to Elida's mother's home in Hälsingland. They had hoped that I would be able to go with them to meet the relatives there, but I didn't have either time or money to go that far. Rueben and I rode with Torsten to Ludvika and took the train from there to Västerås to meet Dad's father's family. We took a suburban bus from Västerås to the suburb of Badelunda where Dad's cousins, Astrid Carlson and Ester Tillander, live. The bus driver knew who lived in each house along the road and would stop to talk briefly when he saw them. Everyone seems to have lived in the same place for generations in Sweden, so it's easy to know who lives where. Rueben says his family has lived where they are since at least the 1600s. There was a church fire then and records were lost, so they don't know how far back they might have been there. I saw pieces of furniture that were hundreds of years old. Rueben's family did not know the Västerås relatives, but they were impressed with Rueben and want to meet the rest of the family. He and Mr. Tillander found out they had worked in the same factory one summer; they remembered seeing each other. The Västerås relatives are more demonstrative than the Hummels; both Ester and 80-year-old Aunt Hannah kept hugging me. Aunt Hannah seemed very sharp and aware of what our relationship was one minute and the next, she would not seem to know who her own husband was. He was Grandpa Carlstedt's brother, C.P. He was a Temperance worker, who died two years ago of a heart attack while addressing an audience. It was so good to learn even a little of Dad's nearest relatives. Elida's folks were those with whom Dad lived, after his father left for America, for eight years until the rest of the family joined him. The Badelunda home was where Grandpa Carlstedt lived, after going back to Sweden, till he died and was buried in the Badelunda church cemetery.

Only Mr. Tillander knew any English; he had spent seven years in America before he was married, so my poor Swedish was again a big disadvantage. However, I managed to stay in touch with Ester for twenty minutes, while using Swedish, and at one point and was pleased that I saw improvement in my usage. I wrote a bit in their guestbook in Swedish and was proud when they said it was correct Swedish. But later, they asked if I could *read* Swedish better than I could *write* it, and I was rather crushed again.

I have been impressed by the ceremony of shaking hands and pronouncing it all right to "call me 'du' now" instead of "ni" I didn't know what was happening the first couple of times it happened, am still not sure I have caught it each time when in a group of familiar exchanges. Rueben's behavior at Västerås indicated other possible nuances of etiquette that I was perhaps ignoring also. Things to remember: a walk through the lovely woods near Tillanders to see the "Judge's Circle" of rune stones from 500 B.C.; one of the largest birch trees in Sweden in their backyard; a photographer arriving to take pictures of Hannah and Ester because they were both Johanssons and this was Johannes' Day, their "little birthdays" and also Women's Week; Aunt Hannah remarking several times about the "fine boy" that was with me; watching the hail and seeing the two little "*sommarn barnen*" (summer children) get excited about it. I left at 5:45 with a warm glow and the feeling that my ancestors on Dad's side didn't end with him, that he came from a real family too—I have known Mother's family well all my life—very nice people who had really meant something to me for a short time.

Rueben and I had an hour to wait for the train in Västerås, so we walked around the parks and shops and almost missed our train. Beverly and Lars Thunberg, with whom she had stayed, were waiting for us and were quite excited as we ran for it. Back in Stockholm, we met Barbara D. and Valborg Swenson, one of the girls from the Diaconate Hospital, and we all went up to the King's Tower again to eat. Rueben said he got us a table by talking English to the waitress? Then it was time to hurry back to the station and get on our sleeper to Malmö, Rueben and Valborg seeing us off. I really hated to say good-bye to Rueben. It had been so wonderful to have had him looking out for me for several days; he smoothed them so beautifully and I had liked him so much. I felt so much closer to Sweden, my relatives, and others I had met, and knew I would love to come back to see more of them some day.

July 21:

Bev, Barbara D. and I spent the night on the sleeper from Stockholm to Malmö. They were the best train accommodations we had had, with very soft mattresses, soft white comforters, more space than usual, so we hated to get out in the morning. We dressed in jeans and raincoats since it was raining a little. We checked all of our luggage except for one small bag, found some breakfast, then checked at the American Express office for a message from Phil and Paul in case they had changed their minds about biking with us. No message, so we went back to the

67

depot just as they arrived. They had gotten us membership in the Svenska Tourist Föreningen, had bike shops and hostels located, and had a trip to Ystad on the south coast planned. We didn't get started as early as hoped because two were to get bikes at one shop and three at another and three ended up at the shop for two, and vice versa. Then we arrived at the corner agreeing with the address we had been given, but no bicycle shop there. It took a lot of questions, a lot of extra walking, and running into Phil to get it all straightened out. Then we all met and stood calmly talking when Barbara's tire blew out. It was especially funny because she had just said,"What if we have a blowout?" and Paul had said, "Oh, we don't have to worry about that. I had a bike for four years and never had a blowout." So we all stood in the street and laughed like fools, while others stood and stared and wondered what was so funny about a blowout. We finally got started at 11 A.M. or so. We decided Malmö was a pretty big place by the time we got out of it, and that it was uphill all the way out. Bev and I admitted to our legs already feeling the strain; the rest didn't. It rained or threatened to rain most of the middle of the day and we were splashed with mud as we biked, as well as having our clothes staying pretty damp. We were glad we didn't have more sunshine, though, or we would have been very warm. We stopped to look at a castle; otherwise kept to the road.

Our final rest stop was at a little town where we wanted a toilet. The girl couldn't understand any of the terms we used; the rest were real generous and said I could do the talking since I knew Swedish. She called her father and we tried all the terms we knew on him. Phil finally drew a picture of two doors with *Herren* and *Damen* on them and stick dolls with skirt and pants. This, together with shouting "Water Closet!" finally made the light break in on him, but some of our conversation in the meantime, as my blunt "Toilet!" to his first "What do you want?" from behind the counter, was ridiculous and it was all becoming pretty silly to be having such an uproar over it. We felt as if the whole town were being summoned. Then, when he did understand, he quickly motioned to us and disappeared out the back door. We followed, but by that time, he was back in the front door looking for us, and we were on the outside looking in. A bread-man was hiding his face on one side of the room, but I got a look at his face and it was convulsed. I'm sure he had understood and was highly amused. Later, we passed him stopped at a side road with a group of women around him, and as the last of us passed, they all burst out laughing.

Later, we bought a loaf of bread, a hunk of cheese, and a can of sardines and sat down by the roadside for our first meal. We had two or three pick-up meals like that and one stop for *smörgås* and pastry during the day. About the time we thought we just couldn't go any farther, the road improved and the wind decreased, so we picked up courage and made it to Ystad about 7:30 P.M., having gone 67 km or 40 miles distance. We found the STF hostel on the seashore, got a big dinner next door, and fell into beds, dirt and all. We girls—and the boys had long since dropped any pretense of not being pretty sore too—didn't think we had *ever* been more miserable. I can't remember feeling worse! My thighs and legs ached terribly and just weren't functioning any longer. I was sun- and wind-burned and felt feverish. The cold sea breezes, damp clothes, and fatigue gave us the chills and there was only ice water for washing. Our seats felt blistered. We were just a mess! I took two aspirins and passed out for nine hours and the other girls outdid me. (Beds cost us about forty 40k.)

July 22:

We awoke feeling rested and no sorer, which was a relief! Getting on our bikes was quite an ordeal since even sitting up in bed was painful. The palms of our hands hurt when we grabbed the handlebars, our arches hurt when we put our feet on the pedals, our seats shrieked when we sat on the seats, and our knees cracked at every motion, but we were in a good mood anyway. Our first sight of the sea as we biked along it had given us quite a thrill—didn't look like a northern sea as I expected because it had a wide sandy beach. We stopped to walk out on the pier and got splashed. Then, we biked around the narrow, picturesque, old streets of Ystad and stopped to see St. Maria's Church, St. Peter's Church, an old monastery, and a historical museum for the area. St. Maria's Church with its many statues looked very Catholic to me and it was hard to remember it was actually Lutheran. It is easy to sense how gradual the break from the Catholic Church has been here, and how close it still is in traditions.

We had two accidents at the monastery. Paul had his first blowout and went to get it fixed. I rode down a steep path and realized too late that I wouldn't be able to make the curve at the bottom and was heading for a wire fence around the pool. I put out my hand and tried to push myself away from it and was very fortunate to end up with only two minor bruises; a scratch across my chest and breast and a tear in my T-shirt which I had to pin together. When I saw the torn shirt, I fully expected to see torn flesh as well, so was most thankful it was only a bruise. Secondly, I jammed the left handle bar into my right groin and developed a huge swelling. It was so far forward that it didn't interfere with my biking and felt worse later when I walked. I suspect the exercise of biking may actually have been good for it in relieving some of the congestion.

We finally left the city about 1 P.M. and had just reached the top of a high hill about 4 km out when Paul had his second blowout. It was at a farm for artificial insemination, a coop affair for the community, and a beautiful place, so we all went in and sat around the yard while poor Paul biked back to town with his wheel. It was 3 P.M. the next time we started out. We had hoped to make the 57 km to Lund but didn't think we could. We debated about which section of the trip we should take by bus—the hilly part in the middle or the last part. We finally decided to ride while we could. We had to push our bikes up a number of hills but felt well rewarded when we hit the top of a high ridge and coasted down at a fast pace for several km. We could see why people might love to bike. It was better than any thrill ride I've had. We reached Blentarp and put on raincoats, and had just started out again when Paul had a third blowout—sparks shooting from his rim hitting the pavement when his tire left the wheel. I was just behind him and didn't know what was happening. He was very disgusted by that time! He and Phil suggested we girls go ahead, take the bus at Veberod as planned, and get reservations for all of us at the hostel at Lund. The wind had grown stronger so we didn't make very good time on the hilly, gravel roads. We stopped to pick raspberries at a thick patch along the road for refreshment, knew the fellows would do the same, and they did. When we reached Veberod at 6:30,

71

the road was the best it had been, and we found the bus
didn't come till 8:00, so decided to keep on for a while, to
Dalby perhaps. The sun was setting, it looked as though
it might be a beautiful one, the fields smelled wonderful,
the villages, poppys and other flowers in the fields, the
cows being milked in the fields all gave us enjoyment, so
we kept going. About halfway between Dalby and
Veberöd, the fellows caught up with us, both—especially
Paul—very tired. At Dalby, we were still quite a bit ahead
of the bus, so we kept on in spite of some wind disturbing
us. We stopped in at a farm for a drink from their pump.
We hadn't found any cafes open so were ready to eat
tacks! We finally arrived in Lund at 8:30, still ahead of
the bus. We found the hostel by 9:00 and they set up an
extra bed for one of the fellows. We left to find something
to eat, stocking up on pastries while waiting for our
smörgäs order, which arrived at 9:50. We were to be in at
10 P.M., so we positively *devoured* the food, finishing on
our bikes. Bev and I got separated from the others and
were angry at them when we got back at 10:15. We were
all so dead tired that we were ready to snap at every
slight provocation. Paul said, "We got away to relax and
here we are ready to tear each other's hair out. Let's all
pitch in!" However, we weren't nearly as miserable as we
had been the night before, and we had a feeling of accomplishment in having been able to get that far minus some
of the aches of the night before. All were in bed when we
got in, lights supposed to have been off about ten, so we
quietly stripped and I crept over to turn out the light. As I
dropped my hand, it hit a table with some glasses on it,
and a glass crashed to the floor. Everyone turned over in
bed with a start, and I stood motionless and guilty in the
dark, glad for the darkness and only hoping Barbara

could contain the snort I knew she was stifling. It was an awful feeling! (Bev missed it; she was in the bathroom.)

July 23:

The first procedure of the morning was to have Bev and Barbara, between them, pull a tick off my right shoulder. He didn't intend to let go. We girls started off on our own about 9 A.M., an hour later than intended. We saw the university, a cathedral, and a museum in a warship—complete except for a deck—all briefly. Barbara missed part of that because she had a leaky tire that had to be repaired. We started for Malmö about 11 A.M. and arrived about 12:15. We pushed against the strongest wind yet the whole way, so it was pretty exhausting. We had just a bit over an hour in Malmö to check luggage, change into skirts, and make the boat. The fact that I had a hard time making the man at the bike shop understand that I was returning a bike, not bringing it in for repairs, and the fact that the streets were jammed with people waiting for a parade or something, didn't help, but we made it—barely, per usual. The boat arrived at Kopenhaven at 3:30 P.M. We took a taxi to the FUM and shopped from 4:15 to 5:30. Then, I joined Mardy at Sihms for the night. I was so dirty and unkempt that I hated to go out there for supper but they were insistent.

It was a lovely dinner, with two Dutch guests as well, a doctor and a hospital administrator. The doctor is staying with them also. The table was beautifully set with flags having our names on them at each setting. What made my eyes pop were three goblets at each place. As it turned out, I think they were filled with champagne (best stuff I've tasted, whatever it was), burgundy, and sherry.

73

No one drank except when Mr. Sihm raised his glass and said something about everyone needing a drink and saying "*Skål.*" We would all nod and take a drink. He made some clever toast the first few times. Our menu was a seafood salad, currants well-cooked and sweetened, roast pork, potatoes and gravy, cucumbers, a dessert consisting of a cone-shaped container into which we dipped strawberries and whipped cream and then smashed the whole works. After dinner, we had coffee and some more liquor in the living room. After the two men left, Mr. and Mrs. Sihm sang for us, sounding very professional. After that, I washed my hair and Mrs. Sihm's sister dried it for me with a dryer before she left for the eve. Mardy polished my shoes. I took a cold sponge bath which helped some. We retired to a bedroom downstairs in another apartment. We lay and talked. Mardy had noticed Mrs. Sihm turn down the bed for the Dr. and laid out his pajamas—such wonderful manners and still so natural and easygoing, making clever "cracks" at times, but managing to keep them in such good taste. They took us to the subway station when we left, had bought our tickets in advance, and had checked out platform from which we would be leaving.

It was good to see our group again, also a number of the Danes—Pastor Boss and his little boy, Jens Kaeding, Sven, Gertrude, Gunnard—and Hans Olson deserves special mention. He had helped me and my luggage on the street-car earlier, and I had forgotten to give his coat back when we got on the car, so he had had to follow the car to the stop on his bike to get it back! Gertrude was so sincere about having had a wonderful time with us all; that after all she has done for the group. I'm so glad she feels that way. Pastor Boss said, "Gertrude loves these Americans now. She has changed her mind since those critical things she said that first night at Sigtuna." She said to him, "It was *you* who said those things." Rev. Seyda said Pastor Boss had been very critical when he first came to Sigtuna and that he had changed his mind, so we agreed that he was probably speaking for himself more than for Gertrude. I liked him so much—was leader of the Bible study group I was in—so was very glad to hear that *he* felt good about it, and we all felt good about him coming to see us off.

I spent most of the time on the train writing in this diary. We had a wonderful smörgåsbord on the ferry at noon, compared events of the last few days with each other, and Marge M., Carolyn G., and I indulged in a game of bridge with Charlie, which Carolyn and I won. We arrived at Hannover at 7:45 P.M. and were met by a man who took us at once to our new home, a brand new bus for our trip through Germany, with a separate luggage carrier behind. He seemed very pleased with it and was glad we were too. The front of the station was badly bombed and pieced together somewhat. We saw many ruins on the way to Annastift, the Orthopedic home or hospital where we are staying. We had a wonderful eve with food, mail, and a chance for hot baths—my first since leaving New York! Our room is lovely with bedside tables, bouquets on each one, clean white comforters. It's late so good night, but I'm glad to have you up-to-date tonight!

July 25:

We had a breakfast of porridge and rolls, dinner of huge meatballs, potatoes, green beans and plum sauce, supper of *smörbröd* or whatever they call it here. We are surprised to find them served here too. I have had trouble with my skirts lately because my waistline is getting quite thick from all the bread and pastry. We toured the Annastift before breakfast, then had 4½ hours of free time—I washed clothes—and in the afternoon, we saw the Hannover Convention sites with some of the German students. One boy told how his mother, who was born in Hannover, feels lost here now because so many buildings are gone and some new ones in some cases. 45 percent of the city was destroyed, they tell us. It looks very strange to us, and I can imagine what it must be like to those who knew what once stood where there are now ruins or vacant lots.

In the eve, we met with more of the students for discussion and showing of the Hannover film, though the projector gave out before we finished it. I closed with devotions. I talked to one boy who got quite excited telling about how each *Studentgemeninde* in the West Zone has connections with one in the East Zone; they send packages often, with goods and letters about their problems smuggled in, invite each other to conferences, which two or three persons often manage to attend. Another student, a girl, taught for six years in Saxony but left her home because she couldn't stand the constant struggle and resistance necessary if she were not to teach the "Communist lies" about materialism, as a Christian. She said they were glad when she resigned, though they could not dismiss her because so many parents were glad she was there and was a Christian. We want to talk to her again. Paul, Frank, Bev, and I ended up looking at the full moon and talking about God, nature, the fall, man.

July 26:

Smaller breakfast today but still no *Ersatz* coffee and lots of butter on our bread. Kathy Markus, our leader for the Germany trip, says she is quite concerned about the economics of the Annastift, because she says they are feeding us better than they can afford to do, which makes us feel very humble. I wonder how many sacrifices on the part of our hosts, in all of the countries, have gone unrecognized by us; many I'm sure. Even their language situation is probably not fully appreciated by us. One of the boys who seems to speak well in English seems to be letting everything go by, and one of the other boys asked him about it. He admitted that "It's so hard to concentrate that hard that I just can't keep it up all the time." I noticed at Tuna-Hästberg that there were hours when I didn't get a thing out of what was being said because it was too much effort to try to concentrate. The Scandinavians, too, said they got very tired trying to talk and listen to English all day. Too bad we can't share the load.

After breakfast, we left via our new bus for Sachsenheim. Some of the Germans were with us. Bev and I talked to Johannes, a very intelligent Dutch-German boy who knows Alice Otterness from her visit here last summer. He talked about fraternities and rearmament mostly. He is one of the first active members of the Hannover Studentengemeinde. He told of a meeting at Lochusen recently at which they tried to have two or three Christians from each frat to discuss problems of bringing Christian influence into the fraternities. He is concerned about the importance of the frat to students today and also about the trend to conformity for young members who look up to independents. He is *very* concerned about how to develop a sense of Christian responsibility in both the students and in parish members. He can see both sides of the rearmament question, but says many are wondering if the Christian has a duty to act as an intelligent member of this society. Some say, "Yes, it may be logically necessary to have armaments, but perhaps God wants us to act in faith as we believe He must want us to be against war." He thinks Christians are always in the minority and even with the best reasons for supporting armaments, the majority is too likely to be in control of the armaments and bring about a new war. Pastor Peters pointed out in the evening that when young people are faced with the ruins of buildings and their families, they are forced to ask if this can ever be right; they wonder what is right and what is wrong. The sermon by Pastor Peters was on Paul and Silas. Rev. Seyda gave a short translation with three main points: 1) God unlocks closed doors. 2) Can you sing and pray at midnight? 3) Yes, because Jesus lives! The German language interests me very much. It doesn't have as much inflection, rhythm, and music as the Scandinavian, but it's so distinct and clipped. Seems as if it would be easy to understand if one *knew* the vocabulary. Even their singing is abrupt and heavily accented: we would have to affect such singing; it wouldn't be natural for us.

After church, we divided into eight groups of 20 each and mixed with the young people here for camps. Ralph, Marge M., Mardy, and I were with some young boys, about 9 to 14. We saw their tents and campgrounds and then sat down and sang and talked. Their first questions were about cowboys and they continued to be predominant. They liked American jazz and that Negroes all played boogie-woogie, so we sang some Negro spirituals. They also asked if all Negroes were good cooks since they are always doing the serving in movies. We explained that some Negroes were very educated, fine people and that they didn't all play boogie-woogie, that everyone doesn't carry guns, that some people in America have never seen a cowboy. Egon, our German student interpreter, added that he hadn't seen any of us have guns or heard us say they were okay. Their leader said he thought our singing of "Oh, De Lord" had given them a feeling of the joy we have in our Christianity, which he thought the boys could sense. I told one boy with a Tom Mix sweater that I would tell him about it if I saw Tom Mix; I didn't tell him Tom Mix had been dead for years. They were apparently missing their swim period, so some boys left, but a lot of them stayed to stare and ask questions. It was really a high spot for us. They all wanted to shake hands with us when we left and it was a pleasure. It seems to me that in Hannover at least, we have been accepted at once, more so than in the other countries. One explanation might be that they have had more contact with church representatives, youth workers, etc., since the war, and that they have had good contacts. This may not apply elsewhere, but Egon, who has bought stamps and done all sorts of helpful things for us, says that he had good friends from the U.S. army several years ago in Frankfurt. In any case, whether they are genuinely friendly or not, I suspect that on the whole, people already have formed attitudes and know how they are going to meet us and don't have to go through a period of figuring us out while they hold us at a distance; e.g. they all give us their first names because they know Americans are informal, at the same time they call each other "*Herr?*" If they harbor any hostile feelings, they may have made a previous adjustment to the situation?

After dinner, Willam, pronounced Villam, short for Wilhelm, Mardy, and I went for a walk around the camp.

It is three very old buildings and space for tents—quite a large area with lots of trees. It has a history of resistance to Christianity. Charles XII tried to introduce it here, but they resisted so he beheaded 4500 people and they say the river ran red. During Hitler's regime, they decided to make it a memorial to those who resisted Christianity and brought in these very old houses and reconstructed them, and put up large stones around it—4500, one for each of those who were killed by Charles XII. It was to be a kind of cultural center. The war intervened and during the war, the church bought it as a venture of faith, the first, I think he said, effort to help the refugees. Some advised against it because of the anti-Christian tradition, but Pastor Peters said they believed that the power of God was sufficient to overcome these influences. Students and volunteers have done all the work. Now it is used for youth groups, camps, conferences. At 3 P.M., we had coffee; then a lecture and discussion of German youth-work and the church; then a little free time, supper, and then we left. We talked to Egon all the way home, about their student life mostly, one thing that impressed me was his saying that there was nothing he enjoyed more than sitting undisturbed in a dark church while his girlfriend plays the organ. He also said that a kiss here may be taken as a sign of engagement and is therefore not given easily.

I can't write this much all the time, but it's fun when I can. There are so many impressions crowding in; especially at being in Germany. Another thing coming from Egon: his father was an American prisoner for a year; he had previously left his home in East Prussia when the Russians came, then joined the German army.

This picture of me at Heidelberg is proof that we did get there, though that portion of my diary was erased from the disc. My husband, Armour, carried this picture in his wallet as long as he lived.

July 27:

Many of the things we heard today are in my lecture notes. I see my attitudes changing quite a bit. I can see again that the "church" cannot be spoken of in generalized terms, e.g. in criticizing the "church" for lack of action before and during the war, we must first ask, "Where *is* the church?" The form may have been deserted but the life existing outside.

This afternoon, we visited our first refugee camp. The one poor man in charge of 1000 beaten- down refugees, including actual gangsters and tramps of all sorts, seemed to be rather bitter, sensitive, and overburdened, I thought. He talked as though his task was an impossible one, and that he was extremely frustrated by lack of others to share his burden. Kathy Markus says help is very hard to get because there aren't many German social workers available.

(*Added in 1998*) What went on between July 27 afternoon and the afternoon of August 6 will be filled in with a few notes here. I lost approximately ten pages of my diary after enjoying typing them up, either due to some error of my own or one of the minor "explosions" my word processor was having before I replaced it after the eighth time it happened and remained uncorrected by Sears repair people. I am sorry to have lost it because I enjoyed reliving it as I typed it up. One bit of Heidelberg has lived with me through the years, because a picture of me on the Heidelberg bridge was one of two pictures of me that Armour carried in his wallet for the rest of his life.

You will note on the itinerary included with this packet, that during the above period, we spent another day in Hannover, went on to the Loccum Evangelical Academy where we also visited the Espelkamp Refugee Camp. From there we went to Bielefeld for a day, and on to Dusseldorf, Koln, Bonn, Mainz, Worms, Heidelberg, Stuttgart, Augsburg, Munich, Berchtesgaden, and then Nurnberg. My narrative picks up again at the Valka D.P. Camp at Nurnberg.

I do also have copies of a *detailed* schedule for northern Germany, Munich, and Berchtesgaden. I am not including these as a whole because much of it is devoted to meal-times, arrival and departure times, but I will include the items telling about what we saw on the missing days.

Schedule for the American Student Study Tour during Their Stay in Northern Germany

July 27:

Two meals at Annastift, visit of the church offices of the VELKD and EKID (Vereiniste Lutherische Kirche Deutschland und Evangelische Kirche in Deutschland), lecture on the work of the Church of Germany (D. Brunotte, President), tour of the beautiful old *Herrenhauser Garten,* lunch at Maschseegaststatte, visit of the Refugee Camp *Muhlenberg* (Pastor D. Petersmann), congregational evening together with the Church Council and Church leaders (Pauluskirche, Hannover, Netastrasse 40, Pastor Knippel).

July 28:

Two meals at Annastift, visit of the Michaeliskirche in Hildesheim, lunch at Predigerseminar; briefings on the work of the Predigerseminar (Studiendirakter Heintze), evening free.

July 29:

Departure for Loccum, Evangelische Akademie; Briefings on German academies (Pastor Wischmanno; tour of academy and abbey; lunch at Loccum; departure for Espelkamp, refugee settlement; tour of Espelkamp (Pastor Plantiko); dinner at Espelkamp; briefings on refugee situation in Germany and its solution (Pastor Plantiko). All members accommodated in Espelkamp for this night.

July 30:

Breakfast at Eskelkamp; depart for Bielefeld (Bodelschwingh'sche Anstalten, Bethel) Pastor Hardt; rest of morning spent touring the establishment, being briefed on its history and services; dinner at Gastehaus Assapheum (Schwester Dora School and Pastor Scholten); visit of the Mamre-School and discussion with Rektor Reuter; dinner at Gastehaus Assapheum; joint evening. Ladies at Motherhouse Sarepta—Schwester Dora Schoof. Gentlemen at Brotherhous Nazareth—Prof. Ficht and Missionar Hopf. All members of the group accommodated in Bethel, 12 ladies Gastehaus Assapheum—9 students and pastor and Mrs. Seyda Bruderhaus Nazareth).

July 31:

Breakfast in Bethel; depart for Dusseldorf; lunch at "Haus der Bezegnng" Muhlheim/Ruhr Evangelical Academy; briefings on the church situation in the Rhineland; tour of Dusseldorf; visit of the Diakonissenanstalt Kaiserswerth; dinner at "Haus der Begegnung," Muhlheim; joint evening reports about the work of the Evangelical Hilfswerk. All members of the group accommodated at "Haus der Begegnung."

August 1:

Depart for Koln; tour of the Cathedral; depart for Bonn (Oberkirschenrat Ranke, Bonn, Poppelsdorfer Allee 96), lunch at Bonn Bundestagsgebaude, tour of Bundestag, briefings on political parties, depart for Mainz.

Schedule for the American Student Study Tour during Their Stay in Munich and Berchtesgaden

August 4:

Depart from Ulm for Augsburg, tour of Augsburg with briefings by Dekan Dr. Lindensmeyer; depart for Munich, arrival at the "Evang. Studentenheim," Aroimstrasse 31. All members of the group will be accommodated here for two nights. Lunch at the restaurant "Kleinkotzer," Barerstrasse (not far from the "Studentenheim"). Tour of Munich, visit to the Evang. Luth. Landeskirchenrat, Aroisstr. 13, briefings on the Bavarian Evang. Lutheran Church, its diaspora and service to refugees; lecture on the United Lutheran Church and the National German Committee—LWF; visit to the "Inners Mission" Munich and to the Lohehaus; dinner same place as lunch; no joint program after dinner.

August 5:

Morning prayers and breakfast in the Studentenheim, depart for Berchtesgaden, tour of "Insula" in Berchtesgaden-Strub, a home for all DPs of the Mutterhaus fur Kirchliche Diakonie Munchen; joint evening with the "Munchner Evang. Studentengemeine" (including a snack).

August 6:

Morning prayers and breakfast in the Studentenheim; depart for Nurnberg.

August 6:

[*Diary continued, after seeing the Inner Mission in Munich, and the "Insula" in Berchtesgaden-Strum, a home for D.P.s. Some comments made about whether we might have been shown the best, some of the problems covered up.*]

The Inner Mission has a kindergarten which looked fine. Most of the war women are single, so most of the war children are apparently illegitimate. I'm afraid it is really a pretty tough place. We saw one fight. [*The following sentences sound as though they would be referring to the D.P. home, which makes me wonder if the kindergarten and all were at Insula.*] They say the men don't want their wives there; one man followed us saying it was really an awful place. I didn't like the air of propaganda at the Y building either. It's hard to ever evaluate such a place fairly probably.

We had an hour in Nurnberg to look around and take pictures before meeting at 6:30 to see the St. Lawrence Cathedral. There were some beautiful and moving things inside, but I don't feel as if the total effect of any other cathedral will ever surpass the one that the Ulm Munster made on me.

After supper, we had a bus trip to the castle to look around. On the way home, we drove around a bit and followed the old walls for awhile. Interesting, but the destruction everywhere is rather overwhelming. Just below

87

the castle is Albrecht Durer's home, which we stopped to see. It's hard to take in everything we see and hear; in the middle of the tour, one member of the group asked one of those horrible questions: "Did Albrecht Durer live near here?" We hit moments like that every once in a while, and it makes everyone cringe, reminds us of other foolish questions we have asked. It gets so that every time one opens one's mouth with a question, one doesn't know but what one might hear about it weeks later because it sounds ridiculous to the next person. But we try!

August 7:

I'm writing from a park bench in Nurnberg, while awaiting our plane to Berlin. We spent the night in a very nice student hostel which was very picturesque from the outside as well. We got up at 6 A.M. again to take a walk around—Bev, Mardy, and I. These early morning walks are high spots for me. I feel like such a discoverer when I find a few things for myself instead of having someone else show them to me all the time. I can stop when and where I want and do as I like; I regain my individuality. This morning, we went to the castle again to see the view in the light, but were a little disappointed because of the haze. We went down to the marketplace and watched the women fixing up their stands of fruit and flowers. We bought some fruit and the woman talked to Bev. We all understood but Bev did the talking. When we left, she shook hands with all of us and wished us a good trip. She said Rothenberg was "*wunderbar!*" and "*Schonste,*" that Nurnberg was historically interesting but not beautiful anymore because all was kaput. We stopped to buy fresh rolls in a bakery shop and then discovered a delightful candle shop for which we almost missed our breakfast while the woman and her very eager little boy brought out different candles for us to exclaim over. They were wonderful!

Later, written while flying through a sea of cotton above the East Zone: We got back to the hostel just in time for devotions and a quick breakfast. Then we went to Neuendettalsau, the "Bielefeld of Bavaria." Our morning there consisted of an hour in the New Guinea museum, a look at the Mother House, a room where ecclesiastical hangings are made, the chapel, and the cemetery; also talks on the Inner and Foreign Mission aspects, which was interrupted for a talk on LWF by a visitor there for a conference. Dr. B.M. Christiansen from Augsburg College was there for the conference too, but we didn't see him; also a missionary who was on a two month visit, preparing to return. I was happy to hear that Emily and "Dr. Heist"—"Butch" to me—were now in New Guinea, It brought them close again, but otherwise I didn't feel that I got a good picture of Neuendettelsau, that I knew much more about it than before. After a dinner of rice with gravy over it, preceded by a new kind of German soup, we left for Rothenberg. This is one of the oldest medieval towns in Germany and one which escaped with very little destruction, they say. It has been retained within its old walls and is really medieval in its entire atmosphere. We saw the Jacobs' church/cathedral and Werkshilfe, a trade school and home for refugee boys, then went to the hostel where we are to stay. It was in a medieval building, I'm sure, with worn wooden steps and stone floors. It smelled a bit but wasn't objectionable. Bev and I set out to see the town on our own. We climbed the tower of the town hall and got a good view of the encircling walls, then roamed the streets, looking at the little shops with their lovely signs in front. There are separate shops for everything here: we saw one for cutlery, one for brushes. We met about eight of the group for dinner in a restaurant with a lot of atmosphere. We sat in a small courtyard with three stories of balconies around us and tried to find a spot where the chairs and tables would stand still on the rough stone floor. It was drafty and I kept my coat buttoned. After a delicious meal, we moved inside and listened to the music ensemble while we talked to Hermann, our German guide. He gave us his impression of the Valka camp and some of the criticism made by the fellow who followed us. He said it was probably partly true—that the half-loaf of bread they get for supper would not stretch for breakfast too; that the clothes they get for 200 hours of "voluntary" work, maybe clothes they needed and had coming anyway: that the Germans may not show foreigners much love, because they have so many fellow-Germans to be provided for and because they do not know why these people have come. Many come for ulterior motives, he said, though it is probably true that the men at camp can legally get work in Nurnberg but that employers probably will not hire people from Valka because of its reputation. Hermann said we must remember that though many of the people there are very rough, we cannot judge because many might ordinarily have been fine people, but they are desperate when they first come and want to find some other way to get along than living in a refugee camp. He thought our informer was too well-dressed to be an honest person, said he could even be paid to come around and inform visitors and spread trouble within the camp; so some of what he said must be discredited. We sat around the table listening, but working so hard to hold our eyes open that it

was funny. We had to be in at 9:00, which was fortunate. I
fell in at 10 P.M.!

August 8:

Up to take another of those early morning walks, all
by myself this time. We had breakfast and a briefing by
Katie on Berlin, than left for Nurnberg where we caught
our plane for Berlin. The plane was rough as we started
down through the clouds to land, and my ears hurt terribly; otherwise, it was an uneventful ride. An army bus
was there to meet us and take us to Johannestift, thanks
to a Lutheran chaplain, we were told. We saw not too
many of the ruins and did see some beautiful sections of
Berlin. The sun was shining brightly and it struck me
that in all my mental images of Berlin, the sun never
shone, that I always thought of it as a dark, dreary place
where nothing but gloom, destruction, and unrest ever
existed. Instead, there were flowers and evidence of a
"sense of beauty" still strong. We had tea when we arrived
and then had a couple of hours to scurry around, wash
hair, bodies, clothes. We met some of our German room-
mates at supper. Mine is Anna Lisa, daughter of a dentist
in the East Zone, who came to Berlin because she was not
allowed to go to school in the East because her father is a
Communist. She spoke very little English so we used her
"Wort buch" a lot; I learned several new German words
every hour and I think she learned more English. We had
an opening discussion at 8:30, got to bed about 11:30. I
was restless and tossed a lot, was distressed because no
letters waiting from Armour, the first time I haven't had
two or three waiting; also a letter from Mother who had

brother Paul much on her mind, perhaps because I am over here where he was lost.

August 9:

[*Some of this day's journalling was lost in the process of getting it on disc. We are still at Johannestift, discussing the constant dilemma of the people in the East, encountering a lot of puzzling attitudes of some of the people we were encountering as the journalling picks up again.*] I went to talk it over with Mieth, a students' pastor here, who seems to think Germany should be closely connected to Russia and that their way of life is closer to the East than West. I don't understand how there can be anything but the widest cleavage here and hope we can talk to him more. An American, Rev. Charles West, gave a point of view I could understand much better. I went walking in the woods with Mary Anna from 2–3 P.M. She seems to be a straight thinker.

August 10:

Sessions during the morning with Joachim leading and doing most of the talking during our Bible study. We sort of skipped around. I thought the most profitable part was a discussion of the danger of using religion to serve political ends, as J. believed Eisenhower does. He has been told, and believes, that E.'s religious sentiments were affected as a political tool and seemed glad to know that we thought he was sincere, even if not allwise. I told him about the group of people praying in Washington, D.C., and asked if some religious trends in gov't might not possibly be an answer to prayer. It has been apparent in talking to these people that Berliners do not get a realistic picture of America because all they hear is propaganda. Their picture of America is of a country which is completely ideal, and the Russians give them a picture of a people where all is false and to be suspected. They seem to have very little chance to know the facts and I feel as if American propaganda is probably as bad as Russia's as far as being warped. The Americans are giving out food here now to the East-Berliners, but I don't think anyone, myself included, is sure that it is worth the possible ill effects right now, or that it wasn't rather selfish and stupid of America to step in this way just now.

In the afternoon, we went to the lake and went boating, a lake where the east zone reaches out to the middle and we were very conscious of staying close to our shore! We could even see the soldiers on guard on the east shore.

We had an evening with teacups. I sat next to and talked to a Dutch boy here for some conferences, who was very interesting, but we were conscious of Rev. Seyda monopolizing a woman who is a traveling secretary for the Studentegemeinde in the East Zone; we wished we were in on it. Our understanding of conditions in the East has grown, I know. I am impressed less with the "miracle" of the June 17th revolution and the let-up of the "church struggle" than I am with the hard-fought resistance of individual young people and pastors and the church as a whole which preceded it. I can't see a party solving the East's problem or getting rid of Communism, but I can see great things happening through individual Christians in the future as in the past, and feel that the best thing we can do to fight Communism may perhaps be to pray for these people in the East who are in hand-to-hand struggle with them.

I was dead beat—Paul says I look like a "licked postage stamp"—by eve, but Anna Lisa was so excited and enthusiastic and is enjoying her growing ability to speak English so much that she just couldn't keep quiet long after we went to bed. Had a letter from Armour and I guess all will be well after all.

August 11:

This is the last day of another conference, a short one this time. The high spots of the day for me were: a trip with Seyda, who is doing a very good job here, I think, and Pastor Mieth and others, to have some *"Berlin Wiese"* and discuss a propaganda book on American science by a Swiss named Zeungt, which Mieth said was not propaganda at all but scientific and thoughtful and was given to him by a respected pastor friend who believed it. The main point is that America is going too far into the secrets of nature and will thereby destroy itself. The propaganda aspect is that it is limited to America whereas the ethical problem remains the same in Europe and other places as well. At supper, I had another waited-for chance to try to pin Mieth down on how those who advocate it propose to deal with Russia in the East Zone in view of what is going on. It is apparent that German disunity is intolerable to him and that he blames America and the West for it, feels that rearmament will only make the situation impossible, that though the East and West must sit down and talk it out, he can't say what might possibly motivate Russia to leave East Germany; admits they have no reason to, and that they will not change their methods. So many things I would like to try to understand better about where in his thinking some of his ideas come from.

I'm sure he has been influenced partly by propaganda, and believes that others have when they differ.

In the eve, we had a square dance at which I think we all had fun, though it was really too warm for it. We had closing devotions. Mieth said he had been more and more sorry that more of the German students hadn't been able to come, that he had felt as if he were at an ecumenical conference in Sweden or someplace rather than with Americans, that he had never met Americans so quick to understand their problems and that it might be because of our previous travels in Scandinavia and Germany. I hope this really has been an exchange and change of ideas in both directions. I wish I could talk to him much more and others do too.

August 12:

We all left for downtown after early breakfast. Five of us went with Kathy to do a little shopping. We only covered a couple of gift shops and a toy store (I bought little) when it was time for lunch. We ate at Nescafe, one of the large downtown better places, outdoors, of course. Then we all went to Truman Hall on the Army post to take the army bus tour of Berlin. Eight of the group had gone to the East sector against Kathy's advice and refusal to take us, which the rest of us thought was disrespectful and inconsiderate since it might involve so many others and there were quite a few unhappy people over it, especially when someone informed us they had called the consulate, who said it was illegal to buy.

A good bit of the bus tour was in the East sector. The Garden of Remembrance, a large war memorial, impressed me, although there was a lot of distorted thinking involved in the sentiments displayed. We felt that everything seemed ghostly and quiet and oppressive in the East. We saw very little rebuilding, very few shops, very little traffic. The grounds around the old Chancellory and Reichstag are growing over with weeds and bushes. Where building was going on, there were three or four men in sight. We kept telling ourselves that some of our feeling was psychological only, but Dr. Zimmerman told us in the evening that the whole atmosphere is different and that people will ride silently on the underground in the East and start talking when they get to the West and the whole atmosphere changes. My strongest reaction was that this was the Berlin I expected to find—ruins, gloom, oppressive air over everything. After the bus trip, we went to Dr. Zimmerman's house for supper and the evening. He is an official of the ULC in Germany. They have a beautiful home on a lake which made Ralph and me feel very much as though we were back in Minnesota except that we were glad to be seeing the view in Berlin instead. Dick, Ralph, Mardy, and I took a walk around the lake for a bit. Dick and I got back in time for ice cream in the living room, then all took outdoors to eat; Ralph and Mardy came back much later. Mrs. Bodiensieck, who is in charge of some of the LWF refugee work here, was there also, and we spent the eve talking with her and Dr. Zimmerman. The latter's views are very different from some we've heard; he says Communism will have to be driven out of Germany by force and that it is completely unrealistic to think anything else, that there can be no compromise. He thinks American food and aid is the best weapon against Communism and that it is doing a great deal of good, that the motive behind it is at least 40 percent humanitarian. It does come through, too, that America really symbolizes freedom to them. We were much less ashamed of being Americans when we left than we have been, though I think the truth is somewhere between his ideas and some of what we have heard earlier. I am impressed with the great variety of opinions we heard and the difficulty and complexity and intolerableness of the situation. I am also impressed with the terrific potentialities we have as a free nation and the dangers to our future from some of the same elements as we see here in our own country—like McCarthy and those who try to stamp out individuality and freedom. To bed at 11:30 very tired!

August 13:

We started off early again to visit refugee camps and processing places. The first visit was to the place where all must come for their initial papers. Not many were there now, only about 400 a day. Many there now seemed to be well-dressed and Carolyn W. was asked for her papers when she sat down at a table, so we gathered that many of the higher class people have left, in many cases the pastor being the only educated person left. The pastors are being urged to remain at their posts, and the whole Hilfeswerk program in the East Zone is designed to keep the people there instead of becoming refugees. They say that where the church is strongest, most people stay, though there must be exceptions and surely no judgment could be made on that basis, or any other, because the people flee. We visited several places, which seemed to be quite well kept now, though it must have been very difficult when all was over crowded. The camp at Tempelhof even now seemed like very close quarters. There we saw a room where there were a number of people who were in the June 17th riot. One man told us how he had been freed from the Magdeburg prison by stormers, was put there when the store he managed did not make the money it was supposed to make, seemed an intelligent man. The stormers had held their own court and let go only those they thought were unjustly imprisoned; criminals were put back.

We had dinner at 2 P.M. at Hilfeswerk headquarters and heard more about their work, and then we were brought to town and left on our own. I had promised to be at Bible study at 6 P.M. and it was then 4:00, and it takes one hour each way to reach Johannestift, so no time to go home, but I was so tired I could have sat down and cried at being so far from my bed with two hours free. Katie Markus and I went to the hotel nearby and sat at the outdoor restaurant and drank a *"Berlin Weisse"* for an hour and talked, and I felt so much better. She told about a friend in the East who was taken off a train and imprisoned for two days on the way to visit her, and had been made to promise to have nothing more to do with the church; she had since thrown herself into her music. She tells Katie that this is her whole life and will not speak of the church. Who knows what such an experience might do to freeze one unless they have gone through it?

We met Gert Guenther at 6:00 and he took us to Bible Study. Mary Ann sat beside us and gave me a very good translation. I thought that many participated and many good thoughts were offered on the meaning of prayer in connection with Matthew 7:7–12. At 7:30, we went to the ballet with our German friends; we saw Stravinsky's *The Fire Bird* and *Scheherazade*. I liked the first best and the opening music did something to me, but the second was very well done too. I don't think I've ever seen anything so sensual. Afterwards, we went to the Valla Fille (*sp?*) or the Full Barrell in English, a place with lots of cozy little nooks. The Studentgemeinde from the Tech. University have their council meetings there. Guenther or someone had fixed nice place cards for us all and we had a very nice time.

August 14:

We left Johannestift at 10:30 A.M. for the airport after a leisurely couple of hours. Joachim was there to see us off, with flowers for Mrs. Seyda. We arrived at Hamburg at 1:25 to find Hellmut Matzat and Gertrude Dorpinghaus (University of Chicago friends of mine) waiting. We had no official greeter so they found themselves with twenty-two people on their hands. Gertrude stayed with our luggage for an hour while Hellmut took us to get registered and he oriented us to the Kirchentag, ours and their reason for being in Hamburg. Hellmut took me to the place where I was supposed to stay, but we found the women had had unexpected guests, so we had to go back to the Kirchentag Headquarters and get another assignment to a room. This one was in a small basement, rooms with a poor but willing couple. Hellmut got us oriented again and then, because I had commented about having had no bath since Hannover, took me to his cousin's place, where he stays, for a bath! His mother and father were missionaries in China and are both dead, so this is the nearest thing he has to a home now. It was a lovely little apartment and in the short time we were there, she fed us blueberries and cream, milk, more fruit, and candy. We ate out on the balcony and the air, bath, and all were wonderfully relaxing! Then we went to hear Bishop Dibelius and another man from the East speak. There were hundreds there and still it was only a small

These are the front and rear views of a small gold memento I bought in Berlin and have had in sight ever since our stay there, most recently on my dresser.

part of the 100,000 people here. I didn't understand the speeches—Helmut gave me a summary later—but I was impressed with what a meeting like that must mean to the 15,000 people who were able to come from the East Zone this year. Helmut says it is so marvelous for them just to be able to talk, to open their hearts to fellowmen and Christians. I asked him what he thought of the food parcels and the idealistic conception some have of America as a place without troubles because they have food. He says that when you are very hungry, you naturally see a loaf of bread as bringing a sort of heaven, that he only knows that the food parcels opened up a whole new world to some of the people in the East, and they don't even ask from where it comes. After the meeting, we went to Hanor Haus below the street level next to the water where we could sit and watch the lights on the water and the light tower of the Rathaus. Things seemed so quiet and hushed and sparkling in spite of plenty of people. We sat and talked and ate for one-and-one-one-half hours and then had a leisurely walk home. We had such a nice time and I felt as if I would like to have stayed up all night talking, walking, and watching the lights. We asked about boats but none were going. We arrived back about 12:30 A.M. My hostess had put her bed in the living room and the shabby couch in her room had a basin of water ready on a chair beside it. She had hung wrapping paper around the dirty walls in the strange toilet, which looked like an outhouse with plumbing somehow installed. It really looked as if she had put in a full afternoon and evening making everything look its best. I was quite touched. Everything in the place looked wonderful after that.

August 15:

I'm writing on the train now. I slept till about 9:30 when my hostess turned on the radio to an English station and wanted to know if I wanted breakfast. It looked as if she were all excited and couldn't wait for me to wake up so she could start doing things for me. She knew a few words in English, but that was all, so I started right in trying to help out with my few German words. After a breakfast of English tea and bread with butter, she took me to see a friend of hers who speaks English. She was a little white-haired lady living in a small crowded room. I gathered that she had more rooms but had taken in four other people during the war. She said she had plenty of money before the war and lived high. Now she lived close to the people around her and was much happier because she could see into their hearts. "Now I have peace," she said. She was concerned about us seeing so much and not seeing the hearts of the people, too, till I told her that we come to meet the people, not to see things and that was good. She said she was a Christian and that my hostess was too. Her nephew in America had helped her greatly during the war and she seemed very appreciative of all the Americans had done for the Germans. She had learned English long ago at a time when the Germans admired English and their way of thinking very much. She and her husband had written letters to each other in English before they married. From there, I went back to the headquarters. to get another map—I had misplaced mine—to get directions to get to the field where everyone was to eat. I didn't get the right directions and ended up having a long walk and eating in a restaurant on my way back. That was fun, too. My big accomplishment was to ask, *"Haben zie an andra gabel? Nicht waschen."* It might not have been great *Deutsch* but she understood! I went back to go to the student rally at 2 P.M., found it had been changed to a place way far away, so had a long ferry ride to get there. I couldn't get in because of the crowd, and it was very late and hot so Katie, Peg, Carolyn, and I went back to a place on the water and had a *Hamburg Wiese* and then went back and sat around headquarters. I was to meet Gertrude at 7 P.M. but we missed each other, found out later that we were both at the spot for half an hour—so I went and joined Paul and Mardy, since I knew where they were, had supper together, then to an excellent concert in the eve, organ and chorus. I especially liked an organ number by Distler, and a vocal number by Bach. I was to have met Hellmut at communion service, but he had had to go back home to preach in the morning. We met Dick and Ralph and had a drink on the beautiful waterfront and then went to communion service at St. Peter's Church, then home, me in a taxi. Want to add that I saw tears at the service.

August 16:

I was up for service at St. Johannes Kirche with my hostess at 10 A.M.. Her husband thought it was foolish for me to go to church since I couldn't understand the sermon (*predigt*) but she folded her hands and indicated that I could pray and worship and I showed her the hymnbook that I had. I find that I can now understand a good deal of the words of the hymns and liturgy—almost as much as in Sweden. After service, she took me to her sister's place. She had worked at a shooting gallery where English soldiers came, and said she had known some English, but I actually found that I used more German than she did English. A few weeks with people who don't speak English would really teach me German, I think, though I would also need some grammar lessons. They made me stay for dinner, a huge helping of fresh mushrooms, fried potatoes and gravy, bean salad, fruit soup. From there, I went to headquarters. and sat around till near 2 P.M., then started for the big rally, 250,000 expected. It rained and I didn't understand much, but I did get something out of listening and watching people's reactions. I also understood quite a bit of the closing prayer—thanks to God for wiping out some of the sorrows of the people, for the chance to have had this meeting. I was most moved afterwards when all the pastors, with their black robes and gold crosses, gathered on the podium and waved to the people and the people waved and waved in return. I wondered what questions about their future, what concern for each other, what gratitude for the meeting were in their hearts, and I wanted to weep with them. Then the people—hundreds—pushed forward and stood around singing for a while. It was very moving. I stayed till the crowd thinned, hoping to keep an appointment with Gertrude, but I hear they sang all the way. There was still singing amidst much pushing at the S. Bahn station. I met Gertrude back at the headquarters building and we had a quick supper and then went to St. Michael's church to get my blue ticket from Paul and try to get tickets to *St. Matthew's Passion*. We got in and were given seats in a reserved, very plush section in front when Gertrude explained that she needed to be with us to interpret. As it was, we found that we understood most everything in the script, much from the actual words, not just the context. I never realized before how impossible to do justice to music translating from the original. There were so many places where the German words seemed to make the music. The soloists were very good. At first I liked the deep, rich tones of the bass who sang Jesus' words, but then my appreciation of the tenor who gave the recitative grew tremendously; the contrast when thirty-three of Jesus' words came in was wonderful. By the end, I no longer felt that the soprano was too controlled. The chorus with its varying harmonies of *A Sacred Head* was very beautiful, and it went all through me. I really jumped when they shouted for Barabbas. Gertrude and I had a long walk back to the Daumter afterwards. I took a taxi the rest of the way at 11:45 P.M.

August 17:

I thought I had made myself understood about being awakened at 7 A.M. but apparently not, because I awakened at 8:45. I had told Mardy and Katie that I would be at the LWF office at 9 A.M. to get my Hannover luggage. My hostess wanted me to go see her friend and her sister again, but we settled for a quick conversation through the window with her friends and I made it to LWF at 9:30. I repacked luggage for an hour. Four of us with lots of boxes and suitcases miraculously were able to get into a little Volkswagen taxi which didn't look as if it would hold one of us. Of course each of us held a suitcase on our knees. We arrived at Altona at 11:00 and spent till 1:30 getting a couple of boxes wrapped and sent. We missed an appointment for 1 P.M. with Katie and hadn't gotten the heavy suitcase checked at Altona Station and my other two to Gertrude's as planned. Bev and I had dinner, after being soaked for 2 D.M.s by a man that was being nice, we thought, for carrying our suitcases across the street; then went exploring a bit. The Art Institute was closed so we went to Amerika Haus. We saw a lot of propaganda, but a lot of it didn't look bad at all. We met two players for the Globe Trotters and got into quite a discussion about Europe. They left, but one came back and we talked some more—till we were asked to leave because we were talking too loudly, so we moved to the street to continue. He was nice looking and nice enough as Americans go, but his ideas and attitudes re Europe were most objectionable to us and we could see why many Europeans must react against that sort of American when we ourselves did. Trouble was, his attitude seemed so typically American in the sense that only an American would be so loud and emphatic in his views. When we disagreed, *we* needed more information; he knew it all; he had really seen Europe, though he always travels first class and has spent $5.00 beyond his $600 a day allowance. We told him if he threw money around, he must expect to have people try to "take" him, because they would at home too. He didn't think he was rich. "Have you seen any starving people here? Why don't we keep our money and feed our poor people at home?" he said until he heard what we were spending for the summer and how we traveled; then his reaction was, "Okay, you're poor. If you like to travel that way, okay! I don't have to go slumming to know how the people live." We reminded him that the people who lived that way with us were University students, not slummers, and asked him if he had seen any refugee camps if he thought they didn't need our money for housing here. He said people here were laughing at America for trying to buy their friendship, and we suggested that the solution was for us to try to understand them as well, which is what they want. To his "Why should we try to understand them?" we pointed out that it was only necessary for us if we were to get along with people at all. We told him how different he seemed compared to the people we had been with, and how much he was like what we were criticized for as Americans when we raised our voices when trying to discuss differences. I think it had some effect because he calmed down and seemed to decide he couldn't tell it all to us. We went window shopping together in peace. It was an interesting, if rather disturbing, reaction to a fel-

low American. He is going to lecture on Europe to Phila-
delphia schoolchildren this winter. When we finally left
him, it was supper time, so Bev and I ate quickly and then
met Gertrude at 7:45. We took a 30-minute boat ride back
through the lighted and exciting looking harbor; it reminded me of *Le Havre;* then had tea outdoors above the
water. We came back at 10:30, washed hair and clothes,
and to bed.

August 18:

Up at 7:15, polished shoes, had breakfast with Gertrude, even got a letter off to Anne Carlsen about the possibility of my sister Mary who was newly crippled, getting
into CC (crippled children) School next year. Not a bad
start for the day. We left Hamburg for Göttingen at 10
A.M. We have been talking over our experiences in Hamburg. It was really good to have seen Gertrude again. She
does have a sure and living faith, the kind that makes her
work and see a lot of things. We heard two reactions
through her of people to the Kirchentag: 1) A pastor from
the East who was glad to go back because people here
were so materialistic, only wanting to satisfy themselves,
not caring about people in the East. Gertrude said he perhaps forgets that Hamburg has always been considered a
rich city but that in his position, he may have become
very sensitive to the needs of the people and feel that everyone should be that way. Katie said it was good to hear
her friends from the East say that they would be arguing
the same things and feeling the same way in the East if
they had a chance, that even when they stand fast, they
often do so fearfully and not in real victorious faith, that
they are often made out to be heroes when they aren't,

that many have fallen away also. 2) Gertrude told of hearing just this morning of Kirchentag leaders who spoke in the streets, had tried to make trouble, and now all areas finally hushed, that something was really felt in the crowd. Katie says her friends were very thrilled with the Kirchentag, especially the discussion groups. She also told of how Saturday night, the whole crowd of youth shrieked for joy when a Meeting of Saxony and its adjoining province in the West was announced. I'm sure both good and evil come of everything. Perhaps many going home with the pastor's attitude would be ripe for Communism.

Later: We had an uneventful train ride except that I did get a lot of writing done. There was a nice batch of mail waiting; all sounded so cheerful and interesting this time—Mother, Dad, Margaret, Grace, Faith, Armour—all better than usual. German students are not here yet, so we just sat around and talked and planned our free time till 10 P.M., had group devotions and then to bed. We are staying at Mariasprings, a 15-minute drive from Göttingen by bus. The spring and brook go rushing by just outside our windows and the lambs *baa aa* constantly; everything is lovely, fresh, and countrified. We are staying in a large building. There are a group of refugee girls here from Berlin too, who appear very curious but with whom we haven't made contact yet. There is also a woman from the East who came here to help but went crazy living on our floor; she scolds at night. They are trying to get her into a hospital. Several people have had colds and coughs, especially Dick and Mardy.

August 19:

Mardy coughed much of the night, I think, and my head seemed a bit stuffed, but the place is so lovely, one can't wake up feeling anything but good. We went to town at 9 A.M. It was bad to set us loose with some free time and 100 marks' refund; I went a bit wild on my buying. I'm about through now, though. Göttingen is a lovely town, celebrating its 1000-year anniversary. So many interesting places and shops and views to see—would love to live here for a while. Ate lunch outdoors at the Rathaus Kellar, just in back of the "Goose Girl" fountain. We saw some University buildings, including the well-decorated University prison where Bismarck spent 11 days, and the library, the only building badly bombed. We had a short walk on the old city wall, which looks just like a garden or wooded walk except that it is elevated. We were back at 4:20. About 13 of the German students had arrived, so we got somewhat acquainted. After supper, we had an orientation session to meet each other. We sat around a bit and ended with chapel services in the village at 10 P.M. I was almost asleep during a meeting of the group leaders afterwards. I went to bed in the dark.

August 20:

My bed goes up in the middle and down at the ends so I had an active night pushing myself away from the head of the bed. We had morning matins at 8 A.M., Bible study at 10 A.M. I led a group; the Germans and all were very good at taking part. It seemed that all of the groups had very good sessions. One thing I've been pondering is that we discussed the fact that there is a connection between evil in a material sense and evil to men's souls, though the two must not be considered identical. It seems to me that if Christians took evil here seriously and fought it with all their might, Communism would not be able to appeal to people from a materialistic point of view, nor would it be able to accuse Christians of quietism and their religion of being an opiate.

Later: Dr. Mau was our first speaker today. The evening discussions with the group seem to be between the pastors, and no one is particularly appreciative of that.

August 21:

We got up and helped correlate between Paul, who was playing the organ for services, and Phil who was pumping the bellows for matins in our little village chapel. I had never seen this before. Yesterday morning something happened and the organ sounded as if it were dying a horrible, gasping death; it was really funny! The poor organ has been quite a topic of conversations since.

One of the students from Halle showed up today; he had gotten an extension from West Germany after the Kirchentag ended. Pastor Dieter Anderson is making a big hit with all of us. He is such a fine, deep Christian thinker and is so expressive every time he says a word, even in German, and has so much fun trying to talk in English—has a terrific sense of humor and makes a joke of anything appropriate, has his own spry manner for saying things. He is leaving student work to become pastor at Hildesheim, unfortunately. Dr. Edgar Carlson is also here right now; don't know if we will see him.

We spent the afternoon free time with Ralph and Mary over a letter, with numerous lengthy interruptions

The group at our last conference at Göttingen which was the only one including some East German students.

to admire Wm. Busch, the leading German humorist's work. (*Won't try to clarify that because I don't get the connections, but liked the Busch reminder.*) It was a rainy day.

August 22:

People are gradually getting out of beds with their colds—Mardy, Dick, Mary, Frank. Everyone is a little tired and susceptible, I think. We got up and correlated for chapel services again: there were a few slips again due to various things. Poor Paul hits the keys madly and no sound, never knows when. We are awakened in the morning by some of the girls' singing with Mrs. Bockmeyer, the manager of this place, who is so thoughtful. As pastor A. says, "She gives the place a heart." We find flowers, candy in our rooms. She brings cough syrup to those needing it. I am impressed with the attention everyone here gives to their shoes; they seem to be polishing away every morning. Four more students arrived from Halle today. It was the first time some have been out of the East Zone for years, 13 years for one of them. The one in our discussion group told us about Pastor Hammud's being imprisoned and his release and the work of the Studentengemeinde. He wanted to ask us questions too. I was both interested and perturbed because Ron and Dick kept trying to call an end to the gathering so they could go shave. Have had some very stimulating discussions on politics with various people. All are very troubled and concerned about elections only two weeks away, about rearmament, about what their vote will mean to and how interpreted by the East. I see great dangers in rearmament but I fail to see any other solution for them and don't see how they live with the realistic facts of Communism. It can surely be at best a temporary solution but seems as if there is a chance in it at least.

I walked to the village and back with one of the German students who has thirty-six volunteers for the army in case of war, because he thinks the fellows will need some leaders who will work to control and lessen the hate and vengeance which the soldiers might take out on Russia. Things like this give us an insight into the deep feelings people have about the things that have happened to them. We sometimes take it far too lightly. The student from Halle also wanted to know how we felt about the June 17th revolution: did we just think it was a wonderful thing politically or did we understand that it has been decades since such a thing happened and did we realize the suffering that has brought it about? It does make a lot of difference if we think of it as an easy rebellion, which is good for our side, or if we see it as the result of deep frustration and rebellion.

In our Bible discussion group, one of the Germans, a P.K. and theological student—a fine thinker—and I find ourselves disagreeing on quite basic points. He sees sickness and pain as possibly coming directly from God, as part of His workings with man and I can't see them as anything but the result of sin and to be fought against. He says one can't know at all how one should deal with this world and can only know about one's relation to God. He sees no obvious connection between one's relation to God and one's fellow men, says separation from fellow men might be in God's plans for man. It is a deep position and well thought out and it makes me feel that many of my ideas are or might be presumptuous, that I'm not really open-minded. Pastor Magull, the speaker of the day, also has an outlook I can't agree with now, and seems both more naive and in some ways deeper than my own. I think it has been good for me to be shaken a little, but I really do believe theirs is a somewhat nihilistic *point of view*—man must lose everything himself before he can be a Christian. And then, thinking of Wilhelm, the first student, "I don't see how man has any basis for action in the world instead of just accepting it all." I must admit that if I had seen as much external sin and destruction as these people, perhaps I couldn't stand to think man alone was responsible and would have to tell myself God wanted things this way for some reason. Perhaps I over-rate psychological illness and quirks and their effects in relation to eternal things, and fail to see a distinction I should see, but I fear his point of view is responsible for the acceptance of much that should be fought. As Lilja says, nihilism is a realistic fact and problem to be faced and worked through here; it can't just be talked away.

Speaking of Wilhelm, he and his friend were hesitant in finding a place to sit at tea; and finally sat down next to me reluctantly. They explained that they were trying to pick out an American it wouldn't be too hard to understand. How to be popular and win friends when abroad: speak slowly and distinctly. I'm sure my record is dubious in that respect.

We had a wonderful *Buntenabend* or (Colorful Evening or Fun Evening). Pastor Anderson was a show in himself. He is so expressive even when he doesn't say anything, and it's so much fun to listen to him speak English. You know he is laughing at himself too, and I admire him for trying. Some phrases I'll remember: "Niceful," "Smoke some fresh air," and "Girl people." Wish I could understand him in German.

August 23:

Bishop Lilja preached to us in English this morning. He arrived in time, which I guess is unusual. His English is very good and he expressed himself beautifully at times. He is, I suppose, typical of a conservative, middle-of-the-road personality in many respects. Margull, who is the opposite and admires Niemoller greatly, thinks this is bad, I think, though he concedes that people like that are needed. After service, Lilja talked to us for awhile at camp. He wanted to know our reaction, so Rev. Seyda called on Charlie, Mary, and me. I think Herr Bishop was perturbed at a selection having been made and tried to start the discussion over again, asking for criticism. Katie brought up our need to keep open to each other. We discussed church unity, which some of our group don't think Germany has, though I consider 97 percent Lutheran a pretty good unity. Nihilism and America were also discussed. He thinks America is showing more of a sense of political responsibility and maturity, that the young people have a healthy naivete not found in Germany. He says young people here show the effects of the war. Seyda doesn't agree, says behind the naivete is a deep insecurity, but perhaps this is always true, only it hasn't always been possible to keep it covered.

In the afternoon, we took a bus trip to the East Zone border. There are two villages within sight of each other, whose people must go many miles to see each other if they can get a pass. Two or three were standing waving and trying to shout to those on the far side of the forbidden area. For these people, separation must be a very real and frustrating thing. I talked to Gunther, one of the East-Zone students, the first part of the trip. He said he had written home saying the Americans here were the nicest people he had ever met and told me that he had felt that it was easier to talk to us than to their fellow Germans. I hope this is because we are naturally less formal. We have heard that East and West are finding out that words no longer have the same connotation and that there are some feelings of division growing up. This is why any reunion is perhaps so urgent to many of the Germans. Gunther had been a member of the FDJ, the Communist youth organization till a year ago and showed me his membership book. It made me feel very strange. He resigned a year ago after he joined the Studentengemeinde. I guess the party changed some, but it was mostly his ideas which changed.

We ate supper at Karlshofen, on the Weser River, had an hour to walk around, and then went home. The scenery was beautiful. The fields are so open without any farm buildings around and the villages are so pretty nestled together. On the way home, I sat in the back with Pastor Magull. I think he must be 27–30 years old and seems younger. He told me about his war experiences—being chosen for a special guard for Hitler; he was nineteen -years old but in charge of a company! He heard of Hitler's death on the way to work and turned back, being caught three times and having to surrender but always escaping by quick thinking and action. Of course he was forced to lie and still wonders if he had the right to knock out an English soldier in a jeep to make a getaway; he liked the looks of the man so much and wished he could meet and talk with him again. I wondered then too, if people didn't have to get rid of a lot of normal feelings to force oneself to some of the deceptions he was forced to, yet he was desperate because he wanted to get away and live like a human being again. He doesn't think he is afraid of anything much since. He was on the student council at his University in the East and wrote for a radio station, but got into trouble with both because of his Christian ideas and had to flee again, resorting to clever, bold methods to stay on an inter-zone train. I felt as though he were almost daring the world to get ahead of him. He was also private secretary to Niemoller for some months and admires his position greatly. He apparently thinks external things are unimportant and that neither Communism nor anything else can hurt God's church . . . because He will always preserve it. I wonder if these people are strong because they are Christians or are daring Christians because they are daring people. I was inclined to believe the latter, especially of Magull, after hearing him speak of his behavior in situations where faith was not involved. It seems to me that people like he and Niemoller would probably not be hurt greatly by Communism, so for them it doesn't matter much what the existing gov't is, but I fear that few people are so strong and I fear for the many who would fall if external circumstances are too pressing. It's hard to know.

When we got back, I felt less tired than usual, so was glad when Karl and Wilhelm cornered Bev and me and we spent two hours or more in the best discussion yet on America and various aspects of our lives: political, economic, religious, academic, upbringing. It was just the right number and I enjoyed it so much. Now it's 1 A.M.

August 24:

The last day of the conference and we Americans all felt that we had so much to attend to before separating. Mary went to town in the morning to get tickets, leaving the Germans to hold down the Bible study. We had the best discussion yet on "Christian Hope" based on I John 3:1–11. Wilhelm thinks we *are* already what we shall be though it isn't apparent. To me, it seems obvious that we aren't, but that the hope of what we *shall* be gives us power to keep on living in His grace and strength. I don't know, but in either case, I think Christian Hope has new meaning for us after this summer.

After dinner, Mary, Ralph, and I worked on our letter for the Ashram. I had many other things to do but I hadn't found time to see the castle ruins, so when Paul was ready to miss the afternoon session and go alone, I decided to go with him. I consoled myself by the fact that everyone else had been missing sessions, but it was a bad time because a number of the others were gone again too, and Seyda was very upset. It was *so* relaxing though to get away. We sat in the restaurant up there all alone and talked and tried to talk to the German waiter and sipped our tea. We were gone for two hours or more but came back relaxed. Everyone turned out for and was very interested, I think, in the evening discussion, which was a questioning time for both sides, on International Affairs. I talked to Johan from Hannover and others till 1 A.M. again. Hated to go to bed.

August 25:

I'm trying hard to fight a cough and cold. I can't really relax in this bed because it just doesn't fit my body; that doesn't help. There was a big scramble to try to get belongings sorted and packed this morning. We had to be ready before communion services at 7:45 A.M. Pastor Seyda preached a fine sermon on the last part of *Romans 9*. Our hostess, Mrs. Bockmeyer, was in tears when it was over, and it was a blessed experience as we finished our conference.

Pastor Anderson made some of his funny, humble, and heartwarming speeches at the breakfast which threatened to undo us all. Katie was in tears for some time and I felt very sorry for her because I know she felt as if she were leaving much of her heart here. Helmut (Munich) played and the others sang as we bearded the bus. When we got off at Göttingen, everyone said good bye to everyone else for a long time before we left. I think we all felt very special about this farewell because it was the end of our tour as well. Bev and I left at 1:30 with Maria Riegel, to visit her in Sommerhausen at her invitation. It was hard for me to decide, but didn't feel we could pass it up. I got my first pictures, black and white, in Göttingen before we left and it gives me the idea of how I will be treasuring my pictures. Helmut and Renata (Winterhausen) were with us as far as Wurzburg on the brand new train we picked, and we had a very nice time singing and talking. It was 7:30 before we got to her home, so we ate, looked at pictures, and went to bed. We were so very tired that we just couldn't wait to get there. She lives in one of the medieval houses right by the bus stop and we were glad to see how people live in them. There were some things still looking a bit primitive and there certainly was no luxury, but they had an extra bedroom, have a maid, and must be living quite well by their standards. Her father is the village *pfarrer* (pastor).

August 26:

The bed was good and the feather coverlet settled down on me beautifully, but I was still tired, and stuffed up on the right side of my head. In the morning we saw the church and town and walked up to the vineyards and orchards above the town and strolled around. We were awakened by and met the G.I.s out on maneuvers. There were only two of dozens we met who appeared to recognize us as Americans and we were disappointed. After lunch, we went to Wurzburg to shop and sight-see. It was bombed a few times before the war was over, because the Nazi leader wouldn't declare it an open city, Maria said. She said it was destroyed in 25 minutes one night, that every roof in the main part of the city was gone, that many had come to the river and left that way to escape the flames, but many suffocated. In the evening, we went to see Oscar Wilde's *Salome* in the most unique little theater, just down the street from Maria's house in

Our bus pulling up to leave and the Germans taking pictures of the Americans.

Sommerhausen. It was in a room in a tower of the town wall. One entered through a little courtyard and walked up an old stairway, lighted by candles along each step. The tiny theater was big enough for about fifty people, but those in the back half couldn't stand up because they were next to the ceiling. The walls were covered with red and bright fabrics with a design painted on in places. A thin net was hung between the stage and the audience to make details less obvious. We sat on cushions on the floor just in front of the curtain. The performance was very good, we thought, and we followed the story very well, even understanding complete lines quite often. I wrote letters when we got home and Bev washed clothes. I wanted to wash my hair and bathe but my cold was worse

Farewells being waved to Beverly and me.

and it was very cold out. I interrupted my letter writing to go down to Pastor Riedel's study and see the 1600s' communion vessels and church records there. The records are like a story book with reasons for death and other details. Once there was an epidemic when 5–10 people died every day for weeks and weeks in the little town. He also showed us a Bible from about that time with hand-colored illustrations. Those for Revelations were quite amazing. One had a beast with the Pope's headdress! I haven't decided if the study is also their living room or not, but if not, there is no living room even though they had a larger than usual house. We found the food a little more sparse than what we have usually had too, though again probably above average. Wonderful soup and apple strudel at noon but bread and cheese for supper.

August 27:

We left for Wurzburg at 8:45 P.M. We took the 9:05 train for Mainz with an hour to wait at Frankfurt. We arrived at Mainz at 1:30. We found a nice hotel (Chrisrich's Hospitz) and started out to shop. The city seems to be in ruins and I thought once again, how hopeless it must seem to people to ever have a beautiful city again and how much courage it must take to try to make a dent in the ruins. There were several small incidents in shops which made us feel that people wanted us to know that it had been a beautiful city once, as if they were afraid we might utterly look down our noses at it. We ate late, washed clothes, intended to read, but were too sleepy so slept.

August 28:

A day on the Rhine! We left Mainz at 8:45 P.M. and got off at Königvinter at 4 P.M. It was such a beautiful ride and we met interesting people to talk to. We checked our suitcases at a hotel and went for a walk, ending up almost at the top of Drachenfels ruins high above the Rhine. It was almost 6:00 so we didn't go to the top. We will all probably retire to an isolated mountaintop some day, because high places seem to have a fatal attraction for us by now. We were intrigued on the way down by an advertisement for a drink we hadn't heard of, so we stopped to see the view and try it—turned out to be peaches, sugar, and wine. It looked as if the sunset might be beautiful and we couldn't tear away. A German fellow came over and we talked for a long time. He knew no English, but by pooling our knowledge, we managed to talk and to our pleasure, found we could *both* understand almost everything he said. Of course he spoke slowly and the conversation was about everyday things. He took us back to the hotel and checked on our ferry to Bad Godesberg before he left us. Since we were on the mountain so long, it was 8:00 when we reached Bad Godesberg. We asked a girl about a youth hostel, and carried our suitcases quite a way to the nearest bus stop only to discover we would have to wait for half an hour. Then we found out about a cheap hotel nearby. After walking for what seemed like miles, we found out that we were in the next village, which struck us very funny. A boy and woman were most helpful and attentive, but we really thought for a while that we would have to spend the night in the street. However, we have a nice room at last, have had sponge baths in really hot water, which took a lot of the chill out of us, and are now lying back listening to the singing from somewhere below, which sounds great. The Germans really do seem to love to gather at night and sing lustily, or just clearly, but always with spirit.

August 29–30:

The records for these two days have disappeared, have only a few sentences from the 29th indicating that we left for Dortmund and nearby Bergkamen to visit friend Helmut Matzat who had met our group as we arrived at the Kirchentag, a German pastor who had studied at the University of Chicago and been involved with our Lutheran Student Association there. Assuming that we reached Bergkamen on the 29, I don't know where or how we spent the 30. As August 31 begins, we have spent time with Helmut the day before. It seems to me that it was Sunday and that we attended his church services among other things. It sounds as though we are meeting him again on the 31 mostly to say farewells, that he had to interrupt our visit for pastoral duties the night before.

August 31:

We learned that the man Hellmut visited last eve died during the night. It has been interesting hearing about his parish. 80 percent of the town was destroyed in an air raid shelter accident, and then a mine accident where 400 were killed occurred. There are widows and orphans everywhere and it is a very poor parish in spite of the rich industries nearby.

We went to Kamen on the 10:17 A.M. bus. Hellmut met us there, and we went to Dortmund where we spent five hours shopping with him as our guide. I have been very worried about getting a new immigration card because I accidentally sent mine home from Hamburg, was terribly relieved when Hellmut talked to a travel agent he knows and half-an-hour later, I had a new card from a doctor he sent me to see. It was such a load off my mind because I had expected to have to spend a lot of time in Holland trying to get one. As we left, Hellmut said, "You've brought the world to me. You know I really do get lonesome." I doubt whether that is quite the case, but I hope he got something out of our stay because we agreed that he is a wonderful man, and that we had enjoyed our visit so much. We transferred four times in the two hours it took to get to Bertheim, once more than was necessary, we learned. We thought we had four minutes to transfer in Rhine so scrambled off only to find we didn't have to, so climbed right back on another car that we were supposed to have transferred to in Utrecht. We were very disgusted

This was the Bergkamen Church in the process of rebuilding when Beverly and I visited its young pastor, Helmut Matzat.

because the conductor hadn't said anything when he punched our tickets. We found a hotel near the station, since it was 12 midnight. An American woman was also going there, spitting the whole way about how America had cried her eyes out for the Dutch during the flood and look how we are treated now, because she wouldn't know for half-an-hour if she could get a berth on the boat for England. We were ashamed of her!

September 1:

We left on the 8 A.M. train for Rotterdam. We got off at the Central station and found the big suitcase was at Maas station. We went there and checked it through customs and repacked our other luggage on a Dart bench, so we could check it all through at Holland-America lines. We ran into Seydas and the Director of the Lutheran youth office, out at the H.A. lines—much to our disgust, because Mrs. S. was so glad to see us. They had made special plans for any of the group that could be there that afternoon. We had our own plans but knew that everyone else probably did too and were afraid no one would show up. We obtained bikes and came back to Seyda's hotel at 4 P.M. to check on who was there, found no one else had shown up, so we made a quick change and joined them. We were taken to a building like the Merchandise Mart in Chicago. It had just opened up ten years ago and is supposed to be the largest in Europe. We had tea there and later a big dinner with wine and all. There were six of us by the time we left them, Marge and Charlie having joined us. In the eve, we saw two of the very modern churches here and had a program and meeting with students. I had to tell about the Sigtuna conference. Contacts were very brief, of course. I did talk quite a bit to Anton, treasurer of the Lutheran Youth organization; he looked like a 20 year old, but must have been close to 30. He was taken to Germany for forced labor along with all others 18 and over in 1940 and seemed very bitter about that. We were glad we had gone along. Rev. Seyda paid for our hotel bill for the night since we took a room reserved for others who hadn't shown up.

September 2:

We started out with our bikes at 7:30. We had
thought of taking the train to Amsterdam and biking
back, but decided it was too far and we were too anxious
to start biking. We started out for the sea instead, stopping at Delft to look at Princehofs Museum and an exhibi-
tion of creative handwork. We had lunch on the seashore,
then followed the advice of a man who had suggested we
go down to the beach and ride on the sand as the tide went
out. We had the wind on our backs and actually floated
for about ten miles with hardly any need to touch our pedals. The fine sand was floating with the wind, the waves
were in motion, and it really felt as if we were floating
too—a most wonderful experience. We also stopped to
look at the jellyfish which had been washed up in great
quantities; well, maybe only a dozen or so, but seemed
great quantities to me. About 2 PM., the whole world suddenly began to change. We saw a dead man wash up on
the sandbar about twenty yards out and tried to rush to
tell someone. Then the sand got soft and we had to get off
and push. It began to rain, and when we got to Katwick,
wet and breathless, I discovered my purse was gone!
What a wild, horrible feeling! Twenty-four hours before
we were to be on the boat! I dashed back to the beach
without stopping for my raincoat, and told Bev to call the
police. I had to protect my face because the rain and wind
were so stinging and in no time, I was very wet and my
hair more and more matted and salty and sandy. I felt
like a movie character struggling along on the deserted
beach, but I was desperate and not sure anyone had gone
that far since we had. I went as far as the dead
man—about two miles, where there was a truck and some
coast-guard men, then waited to ride farther on with the

truck. I got permission to ride back to Katwick with them, and piled into the truck with four young Dutch boys who couldn't speak any English and were feeling a bit silly about my presence, I think. They stopped and picked up gravel a few yards farther. When they got back to the body, they had to wait for him to be picked up, then take him back the other direction before heading back to K., so I got out and walked, getting my back wet this time. Two of the coast-guards came along and one of them offered me a ride on the back of his bike. I would like to have had a picture of me about this time; I must have looked pretty desolate! He took me to the police station. He had already told me that Bev and my purse were there. The man who had found it was one who had stopped to try to tell us about the dead man, had tried to call after us. The men at the station, about six of them, went through my purse, item by item, and seemed to enjoy that; I couldn't deprive them after all that! We rode all the way to Boskoop, about 20 km, after that before stopping for the night, but it had cleared up at Leiden and was nice by that time. Boskoop was a very pretty place and a good place to stop.

September 3:

We wakened to hear the wind howling, so we were prepared for a rough 20 km back to Rotterdam against it. The scenery and towns were consistently interesting, though, and we stopped often, so it wasn't bad. We arrived at 12:30 P.M. and had just time to change clothes, do a few errands, and make it to the boat at 2 P.M. Believe it or not, I'm here: passport, immunization card, and all—and even $10 in American money, plus about four Dutch guilders to go! Already, it is being interesting com-

Beverly and I on our last beach trip just before boarding ship for home.

paring impressions of Europe with the other students aboard. The group this time are more typically college (four others in my cabin), but I think we're all richer and have more to say this way than going over. I expect to hear a lot of interesting things, but I'm glad to be out of diary space because I'm tired of writing in you!

P.S. I read most of *End of the Affair* by Graham Greene last night. It's so nice to have time to read a little, write a little, without feeling that something else is being missed. I hope the whole trip is this relaxing!

The Participants Forty-Five Years Later, as Reported at the Time of Their First Reunion in 1998

People that knew us and heard about the Study Tour group have expressed interest in knowing what we all did with our lives following the trip. The readers of this book might ask the same question, wondering what difference the trip made for us and the people around us. We all said that it had been a life-changing experience. We felt different about the world around us. It seems to me now that it was meant to be—and was—a "reconciling" experience for us and our European sisters and brothers. Inevitably we saw each other and the world around us differently. It would be hard to prove that particular achievements in the next forty-five years were related to the trip, but I believe that all of us did exhibit much interest in people and in being of service to others. We came back and gave talks to various groups about what we had done and learned. Maybe we took more leadership in our student groups. There were representatives to national conferences such as the Lutheran Student Ashram, Student Volunteer Movement, the U.S. Council of Churches. Since we had pretty much lost track of each other, we submitted biographies, which were assembled for our 1998 forty-fifth year reunion. I decided that I would try to give an idea of what each of us was doing by that time in a mere four lines or so, extracting from the full pages we had submit-

130

ted and a few other sources of information. It was not easy!

It was apparent from the biographies that children and grandchildren were as or more important than anything else in the lives of the group, but I will be listing more unique things about each. I was the only person who did not have children of my own due to more than any single cause. However, I think I can claim some kind of record for involvement with children, having had eight younger sisters and brothers as well as an older one, my career was in nursing of children, and young children in our home were an everyday thing until those children grew up and moved away. Two others listed children but not grandchildren. Dick Knudten set a record with nine children!

Here is a little more about each of our lives and careers:

Alice Carlstedt Nelson: See information on author of this book.

Barbara Dippold Honis: New York. Parish worker, U.S. Navy officer, case worker for County Welfare Dept., M.A. in Education from Syracuse University, teacher, active in church, school, sports activities.

Mary Ellerby: Oregon. Director of speakers' bureau at her college, in charge of exchange assemblies with schools and colleges throughout the state. Died in late 1954, I believe—do not have exact date.

Peg Fenske Arnason: Minnnesota. Interior decorator, "all purpose volunteer," term as mayor, president of state-wide society, tour of Scandinavia with church choir, to Jamaica with a mission group.

Ronald Fieve: New York. Medical degree from Harvard

University. Clinical research on manic depression. As: *Moodswing* and *Prozac;* member of World Health Organization, American Board of Psychiatry and Neurology.

Charles Frieman: New York. Married Marge Messerschmidt in 1954. Doctorate in Electrical Engineering. Early retirement from IBM to be Director of the Engineering Foundation of New York City.

Carolyn Gammeter Cain: Wisconsin. M.A. in Library Science at U. of Wisconsin, librarian, district media and technology consultant, all but dissertation for Ph.D., committee for developing national standards.

Philip Graham: Missouri. Doctorate in education, taught at Luther College, Nebr., Grand View, Des Moines, administrator in St. Louis, Sec. to national educ. committee, founded school for disturbed teenagers.

Richard Knudten: Wisconsin. Hamma Divinity School, B.D. at Pacific Luth. Theol. Seminary, 2 more degrees. Pastor, faculty member, extensive writings including 10–11 books, Roger Wagner Chorale, Milwaukee Symphony.

Beverly Lamp Gish: Texas. M.A., taught Chemistry at Arlington State College, worked in Nuclear Physics in Ft. Worth, Tx., research in Psychiatry Dept., School of Medicine, Washington U., St. Louis, Mo.

Paul Larson: Pennsylvania. Doctor Musical Arts degree, Mansfield, Pa. Prof. of Music Moravian College, Bethlehem, Pa., Celtic & Moravian music specialty.

Jane Mardorf Lechner: Iowa. Mathematics/Home Economics teacher, Director of choirs, organist, M.S. degree in Guidance and Counseling, H.S. counselor, church pre-school teacher, real-estate agent.

Margaret (Marge) Messerschmidt Frieman. New York. Married Charles in 1954. Master's degree in Social

Work in 1970, Clinical Social Worker in O.P. mental health clinic, worked in Japan for 2 1/2 years.

Ralph Peterson: New York. Met Birgitta at WCC meeting in Sweden, 1969, married at Uppsala Cathedral. Degrees Harvard U., Augustan Sem., Director Dept. of Ministry NCC, inventive ministry St. Peter's Church, Manhattan.

Margaret Petrea Guenther: Oregon. Supervisor, Kaiser Foundation Hospital, Oakland, Ca. Maryland, Washington, Baltimore Annapolis when husband transferred there. Full, varied church activity, world travels.

Richard Preis: Kansas. Hamma Divinity School, Columbia University, honorary D.D from Carthage College, pastor Ann Arbor, Mich., Normandale, Mn. Worked with teenage European exchange program, musical theater.

Frank Samuelson: Illinois. Electrical Engineer degree N.W. Univ., Il. Maywood Seminary, Univ. of Hamburg, Germany; pastor Des Plaines, Mundelain, Chicago, Lena, Moline, all in Il., ministry to Hispanics.

Fred Stoutland: Minnesota. Danforth Grad. Fellowship Yale Univ., taught at Trinity College, Hartford, Ct., St. Olaf College, Northfield, Mn. Awards for work in Finland, Oxford, Mexico City, Uppsala (Sweden).

Bonnie Zacharias Lebowe: California. Education/psychology teacher, Loyola Marymount Univ. Counseling Center, contributions to major publications about travels from Africa to Arctic.

Seyda, Rev. Arthur: Campus pastor till '55; pastor Nativity Luth. Church, Fla. to '59; Campus pastor Pa. State U. till '70; pastor St. John's Luth. Church till '79. Retired in 1979. Died February 11, 1991.

Seyda, Mrs. Lorraine: Florida during winter, at summer

home in upper New York State, Ontario Lake, where Barbara Dippold Honis and husband also have summer home.

Supplemental Information on the Tour

Continental Caravan—Richard Preis

From the November 1953 issue of *Campus Lutheran*.

Our language problems began soon after we departed from the sturdy ship *Zuiderkruis* in Rotterdam. Pastor Arthur Seyda, tour director, realized it would be no easy task to herd his family of twenty children into taxis, buses, and railroad cars. We quickly learned that on the streets of Europe, our greatest foe would not be the automobile, but the bicycle—and that the Dutch people do not wear wooden shoes.

In Norway, our tour was planned by two friends of American Lutheran students—Pastor Svein Hansen-Bauer, who had attended the USCC conference in Lawrence, Kansas, in 1948, and Dr. Haakom Flottorp, who had lectured for a year at Luther Seminary. During a bus trip through the Norwegian mountains, we worshiped one morning in a church built in A.D. 1000. We were enthralled with the legends of the early Norwegian Church, and the exploits of the great St. Olaf.

A long climb up a steep hill on a hot June afternoon may seem like a method of punishment, but for the Lutheran students it presented a rewarding experience.

Bishop Eivund Bergrav spends his summers in a log-cabin home on the side of that Norwegian mountain. As we sat sipping tea on the lawn, we listened attentively to this charming, elderly man who willingly answered our questions and described his experiences during the occupation. It was in this cabin that he was held prisoner by the Quisling government.

To be the first official American Lutheran student group to enter Finland was quite an honor. Our visit there was enriched by our stay at two institutions established with funds from American Lutherans—the Tuusula Parish Institute, which was purchased with assistance from Lutheran World Action, and Camp Teinjarju, built by the Finnish SCM with the help of funds from Lutheran Action.

The high point of the Scandinavian tour was the Conference on Christian Hope with twenty Scandinavian students at Sigtuna, Sweden. The lectures on the sub-topics "Is There Hope in a World without Christ?" "The University and the Task of Evangelism," and "The Ecumenical Movement," prompted the students to take notes vigorously. Ingalill Hellman, a Swedish student who had studied at Carthage College in 1952, assisted pastor Kristen Stendahl with the details of the conference.

None of us will forget our first afternoon in Hannover, as we stood beside the ruins of *Neustadter Kirche* and listened to Pastor Peters describe the events of the opening session of the 1952 Hannover Youth Convention. The air seemed to be filled with echoes of those days. Here we visited our first refugee settlement. The sight of little children playing beside dirty shacks—children who have known nothing but poverty—will not easily be forgotten.

Mixed emotions raced through the group as our

plane landed in Berlin. We soon learned that this city was all that our host Katie Markhus had predicted. During the Bible Study Conference here, we had an opportunity to talk with men such as Charles West, Martin Fischer, and Superintendent Krummacher who knew the East-West conflict in their own experience.

It is impossible to describe our impressions of the *Kirchentag*. The streets of Hamburg were filled with banners; everywhere the emblem of this festival was seen hanging from lapels and purses. The Church took over the city. An evening communion service with East-Zone delegates; the St. Matthew passion presented by young, fresh voices in the splendor of old, baroque St. Michael's Church; the town square filled with young people for the *Jungegemeinde* rally; sharing a raincoat with a East-Zone student as we waited in the rain with two hundred thousand fellow-Christians to hear Bishop Dibelius' address—such events cannot be put into words.

The final event of our tour was the Göttingen Conference on Christian Hope (again following the theme of next year's World Council of Churches assembly at Evanston) with students from both East and West Germany. In a former student beer hall that is now a rest home for children from Berlin, we gathered to search the Scriptures. The conference was situated only a stone's throw from the Russian border. In the shadow of this barrier, which cuts through the heart of Germany, we recognized the urgency of the world struggle, and even more vividly than in Sigtuna, we realized that man's only hope can be found in the promise of God through Jesus Christ.

You cannot imagine the thrill we experienced when Bishop Hans Lilje drove from Hannover to Göttingen to preach to us on our last Sunday in Germany. "Jesus' words to the deaf and dumb man," he said, "are spoken to you as you journey. *'Ephphata;* that is be opened.' Listen; then return to America and tell what you have seen and heard; witness for your Lord. "

We pray we can fulfill Bishop Lilje's challenge.

[Ralph Peterson also had a long article on valuable things that we learned on our tour, called "Resurgent Church; Lutherans in Europe Find New Courage," in *The Lutheran Companion*, Dec. 9, 1953.)]

Orientation Information on Germany Given to Us for Lutheran World Federation European Study Tour

I. German Inner Mission Institutions

A. Annastift—Hannover
1. Crippled children cared for and given academic training, and training in tailoring and dressmaking.
2. Schools for men: blacksmithing, leatherwork, weaving, carpentering, shoemaking, and making of limbs and braces.
3. Polio Clinic
a. People come from all over for free exam
b. Starting use of occupational therapy learned in United States.
B. Neundettelsau
1. Center of Church Inner Mission and Diaconate of Bavaria
2. Pastor Wilhelm Loke started 1841
a. Trained pastors for U.S. to minister to immigrants here

      b. Background for our ALC

      c. Liturgy from Loke

   3. Motherhouse for deaconesses of Bavarian church

   4. Hospitals, etc.

      a. Care for feebleminded children—1700 children

      b. 700 old people

   5. 12 types of schools, including:

      a. Grammar to seminary for girls

      b. Nursery to professional schools

      c. Pastors' seminary

      d. School for training missionaries (Palestine, Africa, and mostly for New Guinea).

C. Johannestift—Berlin

   1. Educational center for deaconesses, church musicians, social workers and religious teachers

   2. They have 100 deaconesses in East Zone

   3. Train youths for vocations as gardeners, carpenters, blacksmiths, bakers

   4. Many small hospitals—many young cripples

   5. Used as church center

      a. tired East Zone mothers come for refreshment

      b. East Zone pastors meet with West Zone, American and Scandinavian pastors.

D. Bethel— "Suburb of Bielefeldt"

   1. Started to help epileptics

   2. Try to teach children crafts

   3. Theme—"Each man should carry the others' burden"

   4. Care for in all 7000 (2,000 epileptics, 2,000 mental cases, and also old people, orphans, and alcoholics)

   5. Have 2,000 deaconesses in all: 600 working here, also 600 deacons and a seminary for pastors

   6. Founded by Father Bodelschwink who believed

that there were no hopeless cases; when they found their Savior they had hope
7. School for the Feebleminded
   a. Many enter the school inhibited and passive
   b. Task to channel energies in good and useful channels
   c. Language
      1. Taught phonetic spelling which promotes clearer pronunciation
      2. Helped to lose stammering through use of hands
      3. In older grades the children make booklets which help bring out hidden feelings.
   d. Father fought Hitler and saved all of his patients from the death Hitler deemed for them.
E. Nursing and Deaconesses
   1. 120,000 nurses in Germany
      a. 52,000 Evangelical
      b. 45,000 Catholic
      c. 8,000 Red Cross
   2. Deaconesses
      a. Have 5½ years of training, including nursing
      b. Have "helpers", about 50% of which later become deaconesses
      c. They can enter training at 18, are accepted at 25
      d. They are also prepared as kindergarten teachers
      e. History
         1. First deaconess work done at Kaiserswert, led by Fliedner
         2. Florence Nightingale visited here and gave them some guidance
         3. Kaiserswert now has most deaconesses throughout the world (Egypt, Palestine, Arabia, and Brazil).

F. Seminary—Example Hildesheim (special)
1. Attended by students for 1–2 years after graduation from University
2. Lecture to and criticize each other—no professors, only a study director
3. Curriculum includes:
   a. "Practical Theology"—field work
   b. Church law taught by director
   c. Preaching and teaching
   d. Individual study on a chosen field
4. Average Seminary only lasts for one-half year after graduation from University with theology major
5. Three American type seminaries—for example the Kirchliche-hochschule in Berlin and Missionary training schools throughout Germany.

II. Youth Activity in the Church

A. Background
1. One of the missionary field of the German church is the youth, for 25% of the Jungengeminde come from unchurched parents
2. Youth movement opened the door for church freedom
3. Many lay leaders of today were brought into Christianity from unchurched homes by the youth groups.
B. Evangelische Jungen in Deutchland united by:
1. Badge of Jungengemeinde which is not an organization, but simply the youth of the church.
2. Common lecture and slogan of the year—example—1953: "Don't throw your promises away."
3. Common hymnbook

4. Everyone is allowed to console, help (fellowship)
5. Youth conventions, etc.
6. It includes all Protestant Faiths and is much like our Luther League
C. Jungenjeim at Sachsenheim have a youth camp for youth, scouts and rest for tired mothers
D. Studentengemeinde (University students)
1. Task and aim is same as a usual congregation
2. Have their own church services and pastor and once a week Bible Studies
3. *Kleincreise*—small groups interested in politics, soc., etc.
   a. one is administrative board
   b. student choirs—sing in hospitals as well as student church
   c. acting group
   d. mission board who help take care of refugees
   e. medical group
   f. economic group
   g. "eating groups"—get together at eating places.
4. Activities
   a. Freitzeit—weekend retreats and camping together
   b. Summer festival and winter carnival
   c. partner geminde in East Zone (send parcels, letters, encouragement, and try to bring them over for conferences, etc.)
   d. weekly Bible study
   e. Morning matins.
5. Faults:
   a. has lost contact with life
   b. they seem to supply cut answers to questions and leave no answers for men to come up with
   c. have a language of their own

    d. so-called pious ones are the greatest hindrance because they hinder spreading of God's Word by discouraging students with questioning minds.

6. East Zone
    a. 25 studentengemindes and 6 in East Berlin
    b. students have all spare time taken up with FDJ meetings (attendance required and roll taken), sports which are also compulsory and have trouble finding time for Jungegeminde
    c. 65% of youth, however, are members.
7. Religious Education
    a. All official schools have religious instruction
    b. In the East Zone there are formally still religious ed., classes but these are losing ground and being broken up.
    c. Catholics have many church schools
    d. Goal of Lutheran church is to have some church schools, too
    e. Teachers paid by state.

III. Church Struggle

A. Background
B. Struggle went on under Hitler against the Nazis
    1. Now a struggle with communists
    2. At present 28 of 71 arrested pastors are free
    3. Began a year ago when the youth were not allowed to train for positions
    4. Real struggle began in January and February
        a. student leaders and 2 pastors were imprisoned
        b. students in the Jungengemeinde were being given the most difficult school assignments and decisions were made against them

c. Had to sign documents saying they would have nothing to do with the youth of church and they would not be able to continue in school if they did not sign.

d. Church attendance by youth was cut down by having required activities at same time as church service. Those who didn't attend and went to church instead had their names taken and were punished accordingly.

e. Now church attendance is higher, in fact some of it is just for the sake of rebellion.

5. Communists tried to first
   a. win leaders—then
   b. win pastors and then separate them from leadership
   c. then separate congregation from pastor, but Communists could only work where most activity was—students and Jungengemeinde.

6. Reasons for Communists' weakness
   a. Had to take over *majority* churches
   b. Ideology of Communism less confusing to Germans than Russian because it came from Russian soldiers and outside thru force, not from inside
   c. Through Nazis the Germans have been inoculated against secret police and falling for propaganda. The German people have a fundamental sense of truth.

7. Four points involved:
   a. Jungengeminde and studentengeminde are not official organizations (in East Zone) but do exist.
   b. Many youth workers, and pastors imprisoned. An attack made on deaconess. Youth attempted to take their work out of the church.

  c. Church would have been left alone if they had been content with small work but the church wants to work with youth groups, thru Inner Mission, thru the deaconesses the church has the missionary spirit which they will not give up.

  d. Communists want to break the unity of church. But the church has its strength in its unity and its ties with the outside world protects it from the communist ideologies.

C. June 10 and Events

 1. Sudden cooperation of Government to Church: and of the Kirchenkampf with no conditions; reinstated some students

 2. Freed a greater part of imprisoned

 3. Communists did it for political reasons

  a. Determined in Moscow

  b. Recognized that Christianity has great influence among the people.

D. June 17 and Events

 1. Well ordered

 2. Freedom movements, etc., started on Stalin Allee

 3. Political prisoners released

 4. Police in Berlin didn't dare come out until Russian tanks came, but then they shot at the crowds. Marshal law declared and meetings forbidden

 5. Given reason was that the worker's wages had gone down to 100DM per month, an amount impossible to support a family on.

 6. Real reason was a rebellion against the economic oppression, suppression of private industry, and high taxes. The workers had to keep up norms and do certain amounts of work which were of an impossible amount.

 7. Workers looked to the church as spokesman

8. Tasks of Church now:
    a. Must be found in close relation with workers, but they are not overnight pious Christians, though lost mistrust they had. Pastors and workers did not bow to regime.
    b. Must take up sacrifice of those imprisoned in demonstration. Communists say it was Fascist, started by the Western warmongers. Replies of church can speak for the people.
    c. Must orientate their own thinking so good ideological outcomes may occur. Must instruct youth in natural science—extend view in opposition to spiritual Christianity. This year over 10,000 delegates from East of Kirchentag, only 40 last year. Most had not been in West for 8 years.
    d. Pray for the people of East Germany.
9. One of results was the opportunity given to pastors to write in newspapers and speak on radio; but soon only what was friendly to government was allowed and so only 12 out of 8 or 6 thousand did it.
E. Studentengemeinde
    1. Communists knew just about all who were members
    2. Prayed for things they thought they shouldn't have said
    3. They were not allowed to propagandize but got so much publicity because of nature of struggle. Something was in the papers every day, and because of it many more became interested, encouraged, and even active.
    4. The communists had to let down on the Christians as they had too much support throughout the world
    5. They realize Communism is a religion and as such that it cannot be compromised with, must be dealt

with force, and that it will be stopped before it can go all the way because it is unnatural and inhuman.

F. America's Part in the Struggle
  1. American flag is honored by many people
  2. Anti-American propaganda by Communists does not have such a great effect because the people can see the truth thorough the propaganda
  3. The "Freedom" signs are unseen by the people
  4. "The food parcels are one of the finest things the U.S. has done since the airlift." They consist of 2 boxes of milk, a chunk of lard, flour and beans.

G. Propaganda
  1. In films about Asia the lesson is taught that the stronger animal conquers the weaker, so Russia conquers the East
  2. People live in constant danger—that they will come and take you away in the middle of the night and you just disappear
  3. Communists say economy and culture of U.S. declined since Roosevelt putsch with more capitalist influence
  4. Don't say much about American culture because we don't have any
  5. Say we are trying to control the world but the U S only one who guarantees this can't take place.

IV. Refugee Situation

A. General Problems
  1. Large number—28% of the population of West Germany is refugees.
  2. Three distinct types to be taken care of

a. Displaced Persons—Germans who lost home and job during war. (25% of houses in Germany were destroyed in war.)

b. Expellees—People of German background who were expelled from the country in which they were living during or after the war.

c. Escapees—People escaping from the Russian Zone of Germany or from behind the Iron Curtain.

3. Psychological Problems

a. Men who have lost everything often become nihilistic, and even begin to lose their faith.

b. No incentive to earn, save and start because it can be lost tomorrow.

c. Youth don't care about a career, have lost faith in future.

d. Even after they do get started again, they have a different outlook and think differently as result of the past.

B. Work Done So Far

1. Camps

a. Espelkamp

2. In 1945, it was still a wooded area with camouflaged ammunition factories on grounds. The Swedish Pastor Forell got its use from British Government for place to help the handicapped.

3. Small industries were started there by people themselves and neighboring industries.

4. Consists of a planned permanent settlement so that the people can eventually own their own home and shop.

5. Includes at present 500 orphans from the East Zone:

a. Some have seen both parents killed or buried alive and many other war horrors.
b. Most have a terrific case of nerves.
c. Under care of deaconesses they slowly learn to be civilized again and to forget what they saw. Many at first stole food and ate it in the woods, but they soon learned that no one will take it away from them and that they will get enough to eat without stealing.
d. In the school for teenagers the children learn German and other subjects they are behind in because such subjects were forbidden in the East.
e. Girls have a regular household school in addition.
6. All buildings and schools were built up with church help from Norway and Sweden.
7. Once a year they have a cultural week which includes drama, music, sciences, and foreign lectures.
8. At present the camp holds 4,500 people, 1800 of which are employed, with plans to accommodate 15,000 people.
9. The people receive help to build their own houses, and often firms build them houses of their own with state aid.
10. Among the housing projects is a dormitory for 64 students from the East Zone (political refugees).
11. One way to get into the camp is for people to apply for admission to the camp and state their specific profession, and if and when the profession is needed, then they are accepted.
a. Insula—camp for 500 Old People
1. This place is helping to take care of some of

Bavaria's large refugee problem which is now ¼ of the population, some 550,000 refugees.

2. In Bavaria alone there are 7 huge refugee camps but only 3% of these people can remain and be absorbed into the population.

b. Valka—largest of all camps in Germany

1. 38 nations are represented here

2. Both open welfare (same amount as German unemployed) and closed welfare (free living—Just room and board to get by on) are present here.

3. Many facilities including 4 churches, a hospital, movie theater, soccer and boxing, shops and canteens, and kindergartens.

4. Each person from outside Germany coming in will stay here while being screened by committee to be typed, etc.

5. Typical supper consists of 400 grams of bread, 25 grams of margarine, ½ tin of fish, and then for breakfast coffee or milk with bread saved from supper.

12. Hilfeswerk

a. Background

1. Established 8 years ago in 1945 at end of war when people were disorganized and industry destroyed.

2. In 1944–5 refugees of war and prisoners needed help.

3. In 1946 work was started to help expellees - people from surrounding area.

4. In 1946–7 the problem of refugees or expellees from East Germany started.

a. Farmers fled because they lost their farms

when collective farms were set up and run by state.
b. Businessmen whose small businesses were wiped out by the state also fled.
c. Older people left when their savings and pensions and all securities were wiped out and taken away so that they had nothing to live on and yet not a way to earn money.
1. The work was started by other countries such as U.S., Sweden, Norway, Canada, Holland, So. America, and Africa. Then the work was taken over by the German congregations to help their own refugees.
b. Nature of work and organization
1. Two kinds of work are done for two types
a. Social welfare—material aid
b. Rebuilding of churches
2. Two directions of refugee work
a. Through pastoral consulting and material aid, people in the East Zone are encouraged to stay there and not to flee.
b. Actual refugees are helped through Hilfeswerk Centers. These centers are often staffed with foreigners because it is considered a world problem and foreigners can report more accurately about foreign countries. These centers try to build parish houses that will provide study centers for the people who need good literature and accurate facts.
13. Hilfeswerk is the official Protestant organization, not a political one, and belongs to the church. However, it does work closely with the state government in the refugee work. But every church is

really a Hilfeswerk office where collections are made.

a. Present Work

    1. Everyone is helped without racial or religious discrimination.

    2. It is the only organization which can yet work behind the Iron Curtain in East Germany.

        a. In each congregation volunteers are organized to work with cases in their area. In Poland and Silesia men and women of the church do the work of the Pastor when he has been arrested.

        b. Churches in the East have "sponsors" in the West churches which send them food, clothing parcels, money and literature.

        c. There are about 4 million homeless refugees in E.Z.

    3. Work is done only through volunteer gifts, about 50% of which for the E. Zone is given by LWF (most of the LWF money comes from American Lutherans).

    4. Many congregations have made houses for refugees, rebuilt churches, and built houses for pastors.

    5. There are still many thousands living in camps and halls without work. Since only the young and strong are able to emigrate, the old and sick are left for the government or someone to care for.

b. Specific Problems

    1. "Escapees"—in Berlin

        a. Terrific number

            1. In 1949, '50, and '51 about 80–70,000 peo-

ple a year came over from the Zone into Berlin

2. March, 1953, had the highest number, with 48,000 during the month, averaging over 3,000 a day
3. Now the average is 300–400 a day
4. Of the 217,000 who came in, 196,000 went through the processing, 166,000 have been flown out to West Germany as political refugees, and 36,000 have stayed in Berlin as non-political refugees
5. In March there were some 60,000 in camps in Berlin; now there are between 16 and 20 thousand.

b. Political recognition
1. Organized and administered by Hilfeswerk and government together
2. Twelve steps a refugee must go through to prove that his life or livelihood has been endangered by the government in the East Zone. This recognition must be obtained before he can be eligible for state funds, transportation out of Berlin to a temporary camp, job, or emigration
   1. Complete medical examination and certificate of health given which is necessary to go on to no. 2. Those who are ill are sent to hospitals or cared for elsewhere
   2. X-ray
   3. Screen center where political screening begins. Free food is offered here and they have a chance to read American literature

4. Decision whether they are really refugees with a real reason for leaving begins
5. How will they be cared for—where stay?
6. Registration with police
7. Criminal check
8. First and second hearing on whether or not his case is true and if he will be sent on to West Germany.
9. District representatives give information for preparation
10. Political refugee or not—final decision
11. Plane ticket arranged, and when leaving
12. Registered at camp.
3. Those not recognized as political refugees can
c. Return to their previous home or
d. Stay in a camp receiving only a place to sleep and enough food to keep them alive. They are not able to get a job or rent a room until all political refugees have been taken care of and have jobs. Therefore the future holds several years of this "existence" as a minimum
e. World Council Barracks
1. Like a field house project with recreation and group work and religious activities for people in these refugee camps who have no place to go for recreation and religious activities
2. "Neighborhood House" for refugees
3. Contains:

          a. Room for sports and adult play
          b. Play room for children
          c. Sewing room for women
          d. Reading room with as many books as they can get
       4. Staffed by 4 or 5 volunteer workers and a director, usually foreigners
       5. It provides for the people the personal contact they need as they have too much lecturing and mass activities, and have been just a "number" for too long.
    f. Templehoh Camp as one of Berlin's camps
       1. It is place where people stay just before departure usually only one–four days
       2. Accommodates 4–5,000 people, who stay in huge rooms of 150 people or more. Sometimes families are broken up and sometimes many families sleep in same room
       3. They are given a physical exam 4 hours before departure, and then are flown usually to Hamburg, Hannover, Dusseldorf, Frankfurt, or Munich.
14. Expellees
   a. General Problem
      1. 8,200,000 expellees alone
      2. *Definition:* ethnic Germans who have been expelled from eastern countries, Silesia, eastern Russia, and eastern Germany because they were people of German descent
      3. In Germany now there are 500 people per square mile, compared to 51 per square mile in U.S.
      4. These people had to be placed somewhere

when they arrived, so 2 people per room was a minimum throughout Germany for a while ("11 men in one room is fine, but 3 women in one kitchen is hell")

5. People would arrive, 60 in one boxcar, with nothing but the clothes on their backs—no blankets, pens, or anything—and no place to go for food or shelter. Hilfeswerk had to take over

6. Two attitudes
   a. We can't stand it—defeatist
   b. Reminded themselves that persons who come have some ability and are unfortunate people, so they accept them and help them find and use all their abilities.

b. Results of Present Work
   1. Resettled some farms in hands of refugees
      a. Farmers whose daughters marry refugee boys are exempted from taxes
      b. Buying land from farmers without heirs and then distributing it to refugee farmers
      c. Reclaiming land and also distributing it
   2. Expellee bank supported partly by state and local governments to provide security for these people so they can then increase production, etc.
   3. Present state:
      a. 35% of expellees and refugees totally integrated
      b. 45% of expellees and refugees on way to integration but because of lack of housing, lack of money and lack of jobs using a man's skills to best advantage, the job is slowed down

c. 20% living in poor quarters, unemployed, sick, and old that are not at all integrated

4. $6 billion spent so far on refugee problem (this amount is 4 times the Marshall Plan money to Germany from '48 to '52).

c. Future
   1. Three tasks
      a. Reconstruct what was damaged during the war
      b. Close the gaps (industrial and psychological) opened by the splitting of Germany into East and West
      c. Increase the number of houses and jobs to take care of the 20% increase in population.
   2. Needs
      a. 1 million apartments
      b. 120,000 jobs
      c. 100,000 farms
      d. Rebuild shops, transportation systems, and industries.
   3. About $6 million needed each year to care for the 360,000 refugees
   4. Emigration

d. Problems
   1. Have to emigrate all age and type of people, not just skilled young men as some countries want only to accept only specific age groups. (Germany now has as many men 60 years old as 30 years old)
   2. Dept. of Labor is opposed to selective emigration
   3. Dept. of Interior approves some selective emigration

e. Taken care of as follows:

1. German offices
   a. expellees (ethnic Germans)—8–10 million, Prot.
   b. East German refugees—1 million, mostly Lutheran
2. Protestant emigration offices (LWF and World Council)
   a. Displaced persons—120,000, mostly Catholic
   b. Escapees of non-German descent—9,000
   c. American requirements of acceptance
      1. Healthy
      2. Backing of a sponsor
      3. House available for him
      4. Good possibility of a job so that he won't become public charge.
   d. Sent mostly to: (in order of number)
      1. Canada (6,000 this year)
      2. Australia (Luth. church of Australia has 2 refugees there for every one Australian)
      3. U.S.
      4. Brazil, Argentina, Chile
      5. South Africa
   e. Processing
      1. Hilfeswerk turns cases over to LWF and World Council
      2. LWF gets priority on Lutheran families but since it is a liaison organization it can do only what its member churches will allow.
      3. LWF assists with
   f. Visa processing and general red tape
   g. Arranging travel and transportation
   h. Financial aid

1. Use of government programs of borrowing, etc.
2. Combining with government to pay total transportation costs
3. LWF revolving loan fund (to be paid back in 2 years)
4. Hilfeswerk gets original letters for emigration requests (2–5,000 each week)
5. LWF does more alone than World Council
6. Dept. of Labor prohibits any advertising of emigration processes or possibilities but news gets around rapidly
7. Hilfeswerk has 20–28 offices for emigration advising and LWF has 6

i. Types of Religious helped in order of number
1. Lutheran
2. Jewish
3. Catholic
4. Some Greek Orthodox and Buddhists

j. *Our* job—get our churches to accept refugees and sponsor them.

V. Evangelical Academies

A. Background
1. First one built in 1945
2. Now there are 15, 2 in the East Zone
3. The church in Germany learned from America that churches must be more responsible for the *Life* of the people, and these academies are a step in that direction.
B. Participants

1. Mostly people who can't get away for a long time
2. 15,000 people have attended so far
3. Industrial people
4. Non-believers ("I do not believe In God but I think it would be wise to do so").

C. Program
   1. 5–7 day meetings
   2. Bible study, morning and evening devotions
   3. Lectures and discussions
   4. Music and drama
   5. Pastor has personal conferences during the free hours.

D. Locum—Haus der Beregning
   1. Meeting for certain classes of people
      a. Teachers
      b. Soldiers
      c. Housewives
      d. Scientists
      e. Political parties, labor leaders, industrialists
   2. Discuss:
      a. Place of Christ and religion in daily life
      b. "What does God say about our responsibilities"
      c. Problems of profession—"Good Christian as _____ "
      d. Marriage and social problems.

VI. Church Structure

A. Religion in Germany
   1. Denominations
      a. 2/5 evangelical, 1/3 Catholic
      b. in West 49% Evangelical, 46% Catholic
      c. in East only 12% Catholic

2. 95% of the people are church members
3. 5% of Evangelical are reformed, 95% Lutheran
4. Missionary work is needed as people observe only baptism, confirmation, marriage, funerals, and set traditions.
B. EKD—Evangelisehen Kirche in Deutschland
1. 28 Member churches (8 in East Zone)
   a. 13 Lutheran
   b. 13 United
   c. 2 Reformed
2. No common hymn book
3. No spiritual leading over member churches
4. Represents church in:
   a. Schools
   b. Films
   c. Broadcasts
   d. Public Opinion
5. Division of EKD
   a. Group I
      1. VELKD 10 churches (provincial 17,500,000)
         a. Means United Lutheran Church of Germany
         b. Common Service book and hymn book
         c. Established lines for people to follow in daily life, i.e., baptism, church attendance.
         d. Have active Inner Mission
      2. Lutheran 5 churches 2,600,000
   b. Group II
      1. Prussian Union 6 churches 14,000,000
      2. United 6 churches 6,000,000
   c. Reformed 2 churches 419,000
      40,450,000
6. Responsibilities
   a. Main responsibility is activating laymen

  1. now the church is active only if pastor is good
  2. in East people feel more responsible and therefore take a more active part because they know their pastor may be taken and they would have to carry on alone.
 b. Wurttemberg
  1. Joined LWF but not VELKD (the latter they see as a block within German churches)
  2. Want to cultivate religious inheritance
  3. Three reasons for not joining VELKD
   a. VELKD tends to uniformity
   b. VELKD then tends toward self-sufficiency
   c. Churches within it have tendency to loosen themselves with the EKD.
C. Organization
 1. District system—people are automatically members of church in whose area they are living
 2. Separated from the state since 1919
 3. The official ties left are:
  a. Church taxes gathered with state taxes
  b. State pays operating expenses, pastor's salary, and rebuilding costs
   1. People gather money on their own for missionary work.
D. Future
 1. Must preach Social Responsibility of the church (in Austria the people were given no hopes from the church on earthly matters which made communism seem appealing)
 2. People are adapting to our "stewardship" but very slowly as the German people have never before taken real responsibilities in government or church.
E. Individual Church

1. Church council of trained leaders of congregation
2. Chief job is to keep life of congregation active and to bring them together to worship and to keep the congregation on its own feet.
3. Size of congregations is large—usually 10,000 with 2 pastors. Therefore personal contact between pastor and congregation cannot exist
4. Kindergarten work
   a. To make place in church like a second home
   b. Gives children an introduction to what life in congregation means
   c. Helps children of unemployed parents especially
   d. Youth groups
      1. Girls have deaconesses or parish workers as leaders
      2. Boys often lead themselves
      3. Have joint meetings, vespers, and camps.